WHAT DO YOU
CALL
A PERSON FROM
. . . ?

WHAT DO YOU CALL A PERSON FROM . . . ?

A Dictionary of Resident Names

Paul Dickson

Facts On File

New York • Oxford • Sydney

What Do You Call a Person From ...?
A Dictionary of Resident Names

Facts On File, Inc.   Facts On File Limited   Facts On File Pty Ltd
460 Park Avenue South   Collins Street   Talavera & Khartoum Rds
New York NY 10016   Oxford OX4 1XJ   North Ryde NSW 2113
USA   United Kingdom   Australia

Library of Congress Cataloging-in-Publication Data

Dickson, Paul
    What do you call a person from: a dictionary of resident names /
    Paul Dickson.
      p. cm.
    Bibliography: p.
    ISBN 0-8160-1983-5
    1.English language—Etymology—Names—Dictionaries. 2.English
    language—Address, Forms of—Dictionaries. 3. Names, Geographical—
    English—Dictionaries.
    PE1582.A3D5 1990
    422'.03—dc20

British and Australian CIP data available on request from Facts On File.

Facts On File books are available at special discounts when purchased in
bulk quantities for businesses, associations, institutions or sales promotion.
Please contact the Special Sales Department of our New York office at
212/683-2244 (dial 800/322-8755 except in NY, AK or HI).

Composition by Facts On File
Manufactured by the Maple-Vail Manufacturing Group
Printed in the United States of America
Jacket design by James Victore

10 9 8 7 6 5 4 3 2 1

This book is printed on acid-free paper.

Contents

demonym n. 1. (from the Greek ***demos*** "the people" or "populace" + ***-nym*** "name.") The name commonly given to the residents of a place. The names *Briton, Midwesterner, Liverpudlian, Arkansawyer* and *Parisienne* are all demonyms.

2. By extension the adjective of place. It may be the same as the resident name (*Haitian*) or a different term (*Swede* for the person, *Swedish* as the adjective).

Introduction

When the state of Israel was founded in the late 1940s, the rest of the world wasn't sure what to call the citizens of the new country. Some began using the biblical name *Israelite*. It was then officially suggested by the foreign secretary of the new Jewish state that the name should be *Israeli*. It was pointed out that this construction fit in with the style of the area which made a citizen of Iraq an *Iraqi* and a person from Baghdad a Baghdadi. Israelite was relegated to the status of a historic, biblical name.

Israeli worked, but there were many other choices that would have fit in with the broad rules for naming citizens. Commenting on the choice at the time, the National Geographic Society issued a press release stating that the Israeli could just as well have been "called an Israelian, in the manner of the Brazilian, Egyptian, or Babylonian." It added, "He could be an Israelese, following the form for the man from China, Japan, Siam, or Portugal. Taking a leaf from the book of the New Yorker, the Asiatic, the Frenchman, or the Nazarene, he could be, respectively, an Israeler, an Israelic, Israelman or Israelene." It went on to say that even "Disraeli" was a plausible alternative.

What this points out is that the rules are so broad and the exceptions so varied that such "citizen names" offer a field day for name collectors. Everyone knows what to call someone from Boston, but what do you call the person from Little Rock, or, for that matter, from Arkansas? Some never seem to be resolved. The author grew up in Yonkers, N.Y., where most of us called ourselves *Yonkersites* but a few held out for the higher tone of *Yonkersonian*. Mencken noted in *The American Language* that the *Atlanta Constitution* used "Atlantan" while the *Atlanta Journal* used "Atlantian."

Over time I have learned that people are concerned about what others call them. Call a person from Indiana an *Indianan* or *Indianian* and you will be told in no uncertain terms that the proper form of address is *Hoosier*. *North Carolinian* is not acceptable to those who prefer to be called *Tar Heels*, and when it comes to Utah the folks there prefer *Utahn* over *Utaan*. *Phoenicians* lived in antiquity and live—in Arizona—while *Colombians* are from South America not the District of Columbia, where *Washingtonians* reside. These *Washingtonians* are not to be mistaken for those *Washingtonians* who live around Puget Sound.

If this seems confusing, there is a modicum—but no more than a modicum—of order in this realm. Some years ago historian, onomastician and novelist George R. Stewart, Jr. outlined a set of principles for such names that boiled down to this: If the name of the place ends in -a or -ia, an -n should be added; if it ends in -on, add -ian; if it ends in -i, add -an; if it ends in o, add -an; and if it ends in -y, change the -y to an -i and add -an. If, however, the place ends in a sounded -e, -an is added; if it ends in -olis, it becomes -olitan; and if it ends with a consonant or a silent -e, either -ite or -er is added.

These rules work for many—*Philadelphian, Baltimorean, New Yorker, Tacoman, Floridian, Kansas Citian, Annapolitan*—but they also make *San Franciscoan* (not *San Franciscan*) and *Arkansan* (not *Arkansawyers*). Paris (France or Texas) yields either *Pariser* or, worse, *Parisite*. The people of Guam long ago decided that they wanted to be called *Guamanians*, which, if the rules were followed, means that the island should be called *Guamania*. A person who hails from Richmond can be a Richmonder if he is from Richmond in Virginia, or a *Richmondite*, if he is from the Richmond in California or Indiana.

H. L. Mencken was so fascinated with these rules—which he immediately dubbed "Stewart's Laws of Municipal Onomastics"—that he sat down and wrote an article for *The New Yorker* in which he heaped a list of "disconcerting exceptions" onto each of Stewart's laws. He also added a law of his own, which was "that the cosmic forces powerfully tend toward -ite." Mencken found that places with perfectly serviceable names of residence (for instance, *Akronian* for a resident of that Ohio city) drifted into suffix changes (*Akronite*, officially, since 1930).

Since H. L. Mencken's article appeared in 1936, the situation seems to have become no less—and, perhaps, more—confusing as an additional rule seems to be in force: To wit, people in a place tend to decide what they will call themselves, whether they be *Angelenos* (from Los Angeles) or *Haligonians* (from Halifax, Nova Scotia). And if any new rule suggests itself, it is that as one moves eastward around the globe from Europe there seems to be an increasing likelihood that an -i will be added to one's national name.

In this matter, North Americans are not the only unruly citizens. This is demonstrated by the British Isles, populated by the likes of *Liverpudlians*, *Oxonians*, *Dundonians*, *Mancunians* and *Cestrians* (who hail respectively from Liverpool, Oxford, Dundee, Manchester and Chester). Residents of the Isle of Man are *Manx*, a term applied to men, women and cats.

Then there is the matter of France. In an article *"D'où Êtes-Vous?* (Word Ways, May 1986) Don Laycock writes, "Every French town of any size or antiquity, and every identifiable region, has a particular form for designating someone who comes from there, and knowledge of such forms provides the basis for French cocktail-party conversation." Laycock then goes on to list rules "riddled with exceptions" and "extraordinary specimens of Gallic logic," such as *Carpiniens* for residents of Charmes, *Longoviciens* for residents of Longwy, *Mussipontaine* for Pont à-Mousson and *Vidusiens* for residents of Void.

But there is more. In a follow-up article *"D'où Êtes-Vous Revisited"* (Word Ways, August 1986) "The Word Wurcher" [Harry Partridge] claims that "...it is the poorly-behaved names that are really consistent and well behaved because, like so many French city-inhabitant names, they are etymological in origin—that is, they are derived from the name from which the present name of the city is derived." The author points to such examples as Saint-Cloud = *Clodaldiens*, Pau = *Palois*, Épinal = *Spinaliens* and Épernay = *Sparnaciens*.

What is most fascinating about these resident names, however, is that they sometimes take generations to create. A few of them still cause sleepless nights for those people who insist that everything have a proper proper name. The reason for this is that tradition, folklore and custom are in full play here. How

else could one explain the fact that a common name for a
resident of Schenectady, New York, is *Dorpian*? *Dorp* is a Dutch
word meaning village, which brings up the question of why a
person or thing from the Netherlands or Holland is called
Dutch.

Consider the long-burning question of what one calls a person from Connecticut. Professor Allen Walker Read of Columbia University once researched this topic and found an
impressive list of early attempts to name residents of this state:
Connecticutensian, Connecticutter, Connecticutian, Connecticutite
and —from Cotton Mather in 1702—*Connecticotian.* In addition
to these serious suggestions Read found six jocular alternatives:
Quonaughicotter (from H. L. Mencken); *Connecticutey, Connecticanuck, Connectikook* (from Read himself), *Connectecotton* and
Connecticutist. A fellow writer (and a New Yorker) recently
suggested to me that *Connecticutlet* had a nice ring to it, and one
can always side with Mark Twain, whose label for a character
from the state was "Connecticut Yankee."

Although the issue is still unresolved, Read concluded that
the most popular solution to the Connecticut quandary was
Nutmegger, based on the "Nutmeg State" nickname. By the
same token there are many who have avoided the tongue-twist-
ing *Massachusettsite* by calling themselves *Bay Staters.* One rule
of thumb that seems to be in force is that the longer a resident
name becomes, the less likely it is to show up in print. This
means that *Bay Stater* will get more use. In some cases the news
media resort to generic names—local man, for instance—over
a mouthful like *Minneapolitan.*

Then there is the case of Michigan, where the issue was
resolved politically. In 1979 the state legislature voted to make
Michiganian the official name. The bill was introduced at the
behest of newspaper editors, who were confused with a variety
of names, including "*Michigander,*" "*Michiganite,*" and
"*Michiganer.*" Some citizens, however, continue to call them-
selves *Michiganders,* a term that, legend has it, was created by
Abraham Lincoln during the 1848 presidential campaign.
Michigander is also the name given by H. L. Mencken in *The
American Language. Michiganite* is given in several reference

books—including the (U.S.) Government Printing Office *Style Manual*—not published in Michigan.

All other concerns of this type seem to pale in comparison with the peculiar case of the word *Hoosier*, which transcends the simple matter of usage and form and stirs the emotions. For instance, one thing that will prompt letters to the editor of any newspaper in the country is to use the word *Indianan* in print. A quick letter by a son or daughter of Indiana will inform the paper in no uncertain terms that the proper native term is *Hoosier*. A letter published in the April 11, 1987 *Washington Post* is typical: "A Sports headline March 27 referred to 'Indianans.' My husband is in the service, and in all of our travels, this is the first time I've heard the term 'Indianan.' Please try to get it right next time."

With full realization that these questions are not among the great issues of our time, but that they are important points of local pride and proper usage, I have assembled a collection of resident names.

One nagging detail that accompanied this project was that these terms of residency have no commonly accepted name (*patrial, ethnonym, gentilitial* and *ethnic* have been suggested but not accepted). At the outset I needed to give my file a name, so I thought that until something better came along I would label it *domunyms* (*domus*, Latin for home, and *nym*, for name). There were other suggestions—including *hailfroms* (as in, "Where do you hail from?") from writer and editor Bruce O. Boston of Reston, Virginia; two suggestions from Monique M. Byer of Springfield, Virginia: *locunym* (from the Latin word *locus* for "place") and *urbanym* (from the Latin *urbs* for "city"); and the idea from Canadian geographer Alan Rayburn to use the proper French word *gentilé* (jawn-tee-lay), which he suggested in the *Canadian Geographic*—but I stuck with *domunyms*.

After publishing several articles on my collection, including one that appeared in the March 1988 *Smithsonian* magazine, I got several letters noting that I could use some help with my neologism. The most compelling case was made by George H. Scheetz, director of the Sioux City Public Library and a member of the American Name Society and the North Central Name

Society who has actually made a study of words with a *-nym* ending. Quoting the pertinent part of his letter:

> ...All but two historically occurring words ending in *-nym* actually end in *-onym*, and all but approximately six percent are formed from Greek root words.
>
> In other words, the Latin root *dom-* (from *domus*), more correctly forms *domonym*. However, the Greek root is already in use as a combining form, *domato-* (from *domatos*), which forms *domatonym*. Literally, both these combinations mean "a house name." The names Tara and The White House are domatonyms.
>
> A better word for the name, derived from a place name, for resident of that place, is *demonym*, from the Greek *demos*, "the people, populace." The names Utahn and Sioux Cityan are demonyms.

Finding *demonyms* has become something of a minor obsession. I once actually got hold of a Kentucky newspaper for the single purpose of making sure that local preference was for *Louisvillians* over *Louisvillans*. Of late I have taken to writing friends and associates around the country to find out what they call themselves. The best answer to date has come from South Dakotan Bill McKean: "People from Sioux Falls are called PEOPLE FROM SIOUX FALLS. There *are* limits."

Several letters asked me for help, including one from a resident of Sanibel Island, Florida, who wanted to know if she was a *Sanibelian*, *Sanibelyan*, or a *Sanibelan*. The author of a letter to the *Elmira* (N.Y.) *Star-Gazette*, Geof Huth, wrote of the dilemma of living in Horseheads, N.Y.: "I've been living in Horseheads for over a year, but I haven't heard anyone use a word that means 'someone from Horseheads.' What could that word possibly be?"

As it became apparent that there was no central source of these geographical names, the collection seemed to take on a new cast. Why not use it as the basis for a full-fledged reference book on the subject?

But a few anecdotes do not a reference book make, so I decided to approach it in a comprehensive manner by relying on a variety of sources. These ranged from such entities as the State Department and Central Intelligence Agency, which have grappled with the issue officially, to newspapers and newspaper editors, who have dealt with it locally. After all, if the *Cedar Rapids* (Iowa) *Gazette* uses the term *Cedar Rapidian* to describe its subscribers, there is no need to look any further.

A major source of information in this question was the Tamony Collection at the Western Historical Manuscript Collection at the University of Missouri. This is the nation's prime archive of unconventional American English—slang, jargon and regionalisms—and brims with references bearing directly on this project. I have also solicited letters from linguists, folklorists, and residents of far-flung spots on the globe. One of the reasons for all of this correspondence was to get a sense of what term is preferred and used locally. The principle at work here is that of "home rule." If the people of Albany, N.Y., choose to be known as *Albanians*, so be it, even though their choice tends to confuse the residents of that city with the people of far-off Albania. This makes the neologism *demonym* all the more appropriate, because it stems from the same root as "democratic."

Despite this, it must be pointed out that many of the *demonyms* from non-English-speaking areas are also *exonyms*, a long-accepted term for a place name given by a foreigner that does not correspond to the native name. In English, the names Naples and Vienna are *exonyms* because in Italy and Austria those places are called Napoli and Wien. In fact, Italy and Austria are *exonyms* for Italia and Österreich.

Periodically, an effort is launched to iron out these inconsistencies but it never seems to work. The problem was demonstrated in 1967 when the United Nations held a conference on name standardization in Geneva, which, depending on where a delegate came from, was called, Genf, Genève, Ginevra, Geneva and Ginebra. This collection is unabashedly exonymic and does not attempt to propose any reforms. It hereby acknowledges the fact that *Barcelonians* are *Barceloneses* in Barcelona and Bogotá but not in London or New York.

The one great exception to this English-speaking *exonymia* are French demonyms. The reason for this is not clear; perhaps it has something to do with a custom that began because of the nearness of England to France. The French examples also tend to be among the most complex, so they may have held a particular fascination for tourists, travel writers and Francophiles.

What has emerged from this effort is a reference book meant to be used by those who want to find the proper form—or forms—of address. And, if one accepts the conclusion that people do care about what they are called, whether it be in person or in print, then the collection should be useful. I was once told by an executive of a dictionary company that one of the great services a reference book can accomplish is to help people "keep egg off their face." This collection was assembled with that worthy premise in mind.

Special Thanks

A full list of helpers appears at the end of the book, but several individuals contributed so much to this effort that it would be impolite not to acknowledge their contribution here and now. The first is researcher and *Houstonian* Charles D. Poe, who located and annotated hundreds of written examples. The second is Senior Manuscript Specialist Randy Robert of the University of Missouri, who dug up additional hundreds of examples from the aforementioned Tamony Collection. The third is *Londoner* Denys Parsons, who scouted terms throughout the rest of the English-speaking world. *Queenslander* Bill Scott helped with the Australian examples, *Ontarian* Jay Ames with Canadian names and nicknames, and *Texan* C. F. Eckhardt guided the author through the complexity of Lone Star labels.

These individuals along with many other helpers put the flesh on the bones of this project.

Two outside experts Dr. Reinhold Aman, editor of *Maledicta*, and Ross Eckler, editor of *Word Ways*, were kind enough to read through the original manuscript, finding major and minor errors. I cannot thank them enough for this help.

How to Use This Book

The book is organized in simple dictionary form in which all *demonyms* are italicized. Most entries are for the place rather than the *demonym*. One finds what a resident of Los Angeles is called by looking under Los Angeles. In addition, some italicized *demonyms* are listed as separate entries. These are the *demonyms* or terms of residence that do *not* conform directly to the name of the place. *Angeleno* is listed (as a resident of Los Angeles) because it does not conform with the name of the place, just as *Yankee* (for a *New Englander*) rates a separate entry. The number of these entries is much smaller as they list only those terms that are not derivative or are derivatives that deviate from the first three letters (four in more complicated cases) of the name of the place; hence *New Yorker* is not listed but *Bengalee* is because it differs from the beginning of *Bang*ladesh.

While most entries are short and to the point, others include discussions that put them into a larger social context, especially those that have created controversy and debate. Terms that are not derivative of their place—*Sooner, Tar Heel,* etc.—are discussed in terms of their etymology.

The criteria used to decide what to include were simple and subjective: (1) To deal with all nations, major cities, states of the Union and Canadian provinces. (2) To deal with small places that pose unusual problems (what do you call residents of the French village of Y?) or that are small but noteworthy (there is, for example, an entry for the Pitcairn Islands, which at last count, had only 48 residents but is often written about, because those 48 souls descend from the crew of the HMS *Bounty* that mutinied about 200 years ago). There are so many unusual French examples that only the more important and unusual of these could be listed. Fortunately, these French examples are fully demonstrated in the *Larousse* dictionaries (the *Petit Larousse* contains more than 700).

Although the book shies away from the ethnic slurs, it does include slurs, slang and nicknames based on geography. Inevitably, this includes some terms like *Okie, Cracker, Canuck,* and *Herring Choker* that are regarded—or can be regarded in certain contexts—as derogatory. The idea here is not to offend anyone or venerate mean slurs but rather to put such terms in context and give the reader some idea of if and when they are offensive. For an exploration of how a term becomes a slur, see the long entry under *Dutch*.

Although the bulk of the words in the books are nouns, an attempt has been made to list adjectives of nationality that differ from the noun, such as in this entry:

Burundi (Republic of Burundi). *Burundian*. Adjective: *Burundi*.

This sample also illustrates the fact that common names are listed (Burundi) with the official name of the country following (Republic of Burundi) if the official name is different from the common name.

In addition, some common nicknames have been included to add to the reference value of the book. It would, for instance, be misleading to discuss the names *New Yorker* and New York City and not mention the Big Apple and Gotham. State nicknames, even those that have become archaic, are listed for the same reason. Similarly, some derivative forms of place names are listed and explained. The terms *Africana* and *Africanist*, for instance, appear under the Africa entry.

In the same vein, places whose names have changed since World War II have been annotated to include the former name. Selected obsolete names are included, as well as some generic terms on the order of *citizen, resident, native* and *exurbanite*. Planetary adjectives have been included. This was not done just because they were interesting entries but for the practical reason that they have already provided their share of controversy, such as can be seen under the entry for the planet Venus.

There are also some entries that a more highly disciplined compiler might have left out as not being absolutely true to the species in question. However, it was reasoned that these were the terms that were very likely to be confused with the real thing, and that it was a good place to enter them as linguistic bonuses. Therefore there will be an occasional impure entry on the order of *Hoya, Pennsylvania Dutch* and *Utopia*.

Finally, it should be pointed out that while the overwhelming majority of the entries that follow are short and direct, a half-dozen large essay-style entries that appear here are detailed case studies, which are included to explore the dynamics of geographic nouns of person and geographic adjectives. These entries are those for Connecticut (a complex case of reluctant demonym-giving), Texas (for multiple names with historic distinctions), the aforementioned case of *Dutch* as a slur, the nickname *Hoosier* (and the passions it invokes) and the fascinating case of Earth, which takes us into the business of what one calls an inhabitant of the home planet. Also, anyone looking for a small collection of humorous and playful demonyms to browse through should check the case study entitled *Bunnies*.

A

Aaland Islands, Finland. *Aalander.*

Aberdeen, Scotland, UK. *Aberdonian.* Residents of Aberdeen, Washington, use the same demonym.

Abilene, Texas, USA. *Abilenian.*

Abu Dhabi (One of the United Arab Emirates). *Emirian.*

Abyssinia. *Abyssinian.*

Acadia. *Acadian.* Acadia was the earlier name of Nova Scotia. Also, synonymous with *Cajun.*

Accident, Maryland, USA. *Accidentals* (according to a profile of this small town, the only place so named in the United States, appearing in the *Washington Post*, May 5, 1985).

Accra, Ghana. Although the demonym would seem to be *Accran*, it is listed as *Gas* in *Liverpudlian*, published by the Marquis Bibliographic Library. This fact is confirmed by the Embassy of Ghana in Washington, D.C.

Afghanistan (Democratic Republic of Afghanistan). *Afghan.* The term *Afghanistaner* has appeared in print, but it is a rarity without wide support. A demonstrator at a 1987 Oliver North rally was quoted in the November 6 *National Review* saying, "When was the last time you went to the Soviet embassy to protest the slaughter of Afghanistaners?" The adjective is either *Afghani* ("Afghani official denies chemical warfare," headline in April 16, 1987 *Washington Times*) or *Afghan.*

A curious derivative is a word that has a long history in the newspaper business: *Afghanistanism.* Since before World War II it means an excessive interest in foreign affairs, or as Turner Catledge, former executive editor of the *New York Times* explained in 1980, "a criticism of the coverage of far-off places at the expense of local news." Murry Marder of the *Washington Post* was quoted in the same article ((*San Francisco Examiner*, January 27, 1980. Peter Tamony) with this definition: "...writing about a place or subject so offbeat, that nobody knows if you're right or wrong." The term seems to have lost its relevance after Soviet troops moved into Afghanistan in late 1979.

Africa. *African.* At one point *Afric* was a common adjective form of the word, but it has been displaced by *African.* Interesting derivatives include *Africana* for lore and culture ("He was stuffed, crammed, chock full of *Africana...* " Robert Ruark in *The Honey Badger*) and *Africanist* for one who studies African languages and cultures or who forges a strong bond with the continent (David Robinson, son of baseball great Jackie Robinson is quoted in the August 6, 1987 *Houston Chronicle* as saying, "My father was not a great Africanist").

In late 1988 the Rev. Jesse Jackson announced that the name *African American* was what a large number of black Americans preferred to be called (62% of the respondents to a call-in survey taken by the *Chicago Sun-Times* said they preferred that name to "black"). It was argued that the name suggested the roots present in parallel names like *Chinese Americans* and *American Indians.*

Aggie. Student or graduate of Texas A&M University. Female students and alumnae are sometimes called *Maggies.* Though this is what A&M students call themselves, the term is used derogatorily in the context of a never-ending series of "Aggie jokes" in which the A&M student is depicted as hopelessly inept—for example, "Did you hear about the Aggie who lost his job as an elevator operator? He couldn't learn the route."

Texas writer C. F. Eckhardt adds that there is also a geographical aspect to this term: "Anyone from a fifty mile radius of Bryan and College Station is automatically an Aggie, from Texas Agricultural and Mechanical College (now Texas A&M University), which started as a cow college at a whistlestop train station called College Station, down in the blackland of the Brazos bottom."

Aire-sur-L'Adour, France. *Aturin*.

Aix-en-Provence, France. *Aixois* or *Aquisextain*.

Aix-les-Bains, France. *Aixois*.

Aixois. Resident of either Aix-les-Bains or Aix-en-Provence, France. However, people from Aix-en-Provence are also called *Aquisextains*.

Ajman (One of the United Arab Emirates). *Emirian*.

Akron, Ohio, USA. *Akronite*. (The term fosters its share of local word play. Akronite C. H. Fleming wrote to the author to point out that "anyone born and raised in Akron is obviously an Akronite, but someone that had moved to Akron from elsewhere—and remained—should be considered an anachronism".)

Alabama (state), **USA**. *Alabamian* or *Alabaman*. In their *Harper Dictionary of Contemporary Usage*, William and Mary Morris say that "natives of Alabama overwhelmingly prefer *Alabamian*." They add, "Indeed, the editor of the *Dothan* (Alabama) *Eagle* went on record with this statement: 'If there is any merit in the rule of spelling a proper name just as the possessor spells it, then we are *Alabamians*.'" Most citations show *Alabamian*, though it is possible to find an occasional *Alabaman* in print (in the *Whisper of the Axe*, Richard Condon refers to a "conversation between a Vermonter and an Alabaman." Charles D. Poe).

Traditional nicknames include *Lizard*, *Yallerhammer* and *Yellowhammer*. These traditional nicknames and many of those that follow are listed in Lester V. Berrey and Melvin Van Bark's monumental *American Thesaurus of Slang*, which contains an important section on slang "inhabitants."
COMMON NICKNAMES: Heart of Dixie, Yellowhammer and Cotton State.

Alaska (state), **USA**. *Alaskan*.
COMMON NICKNAME: The El Dorado of the North.

Albania (People's Socialist Republic of Albania). *Albanian*.

Albany, New York, USA. *Albanian*. Robert Joseph Powers of Shreveport wrote to this demonymist to recall, "Many years ago an acquaintance of mine remarked that, on moving there, he was struck by a sign in the display window of a downtown edifice: '20,000 Albanians Bank Here.' He spent some time marveling over the size of this unique ethnic group before the light turned."

Alberta (province), **Canada**. *Albertan*.

Albuquerque, New Mexico, USA. *Albuquerquean*.

Alexandria, Virginia, USA. *Alexandrian*.

Algeria (Democratic and Popular Republic of Algeria). *Algerian*.

Algiers, Algeria. *Algerois* or *Algerine*.

Allegheny Region, USA. *Allegenian* is traditional but *Alleghenian* is now common in print. The term is used throughout the region—for instance, the weekly newspaper in Cumberland, Maryland, was once *The Alleganian*.

Allentown, Pennsylvania, USA. *Allentonian.*

Alton, Illinois, USA. *Altonian.*

Amarillo, Texas, USA. *Amarilloan.*

Amazon River Region. *Amazonian.*

American. Resident of the United States. The name has long irked those who think that *American* should cover anyone from North to South America; however, the practice is so deeply rooted that it is hard to imagine it changing. It has become institutionalized in terms like American people, American embassy, American League, and AT&T. See entry for United States, which lists some of the alternative terms that have been suggested.

American as an adjective shows up in constructions ranging from American cheese to American plan and in such derivatives as *Americana* and *Americanize.*

See also entries for Africa (for discussion of *African American*) **hyphenated Americans, North America, United States** and *Vespuccian.*

Ameropean. Blend of *American + European* for an American expatriate living in Europe. The term is little used today but experienced a vogue in the late 1960s with the publication of *Another Way of Living* by John Bainbridge, which profiled 44 Americans living in Europe. Bainbridge used the term *Ameropean* and it was widely quoted.

Amityville, New York, USA. *Amityvillian.*

Amsterdam, Netherlands. *Amsterdamer* or *Amsterdammer.*

Anaheim, California, USA. *Anaheimer.*

Andalusia, Spain. *Andalusian.* A slang alternative is *Andaloo* (a story by Holly Roth, "The Spy Who Was So Obvious," in *Ellery Queen's 20th Anniversary Annual*, speaks of *Gibraltarians* who speak Spanish with "a strong Andaloo accent." Charles D. Poe).

Andes Mountain Region, South America. *Andean*.

Andorra (The Principality of Andorra/The Valleys of Andorra). *Andorran*.

Angeleno. Resident of Los Angeles. *Angelino* appears on occasion but is clearly without significant support.

Anglo-. Prefix that has come to mean English in such terms as Anglo-American, Anglo-Indian, Anglo-Irish and Anglo-Catholic. It is also used in words like Anglomania, Anglophile.
   Among Hispanics in the Southwest, a term for all whites—like gringo, though not necessarily derogatory.

Angola (People's Republic of Angola). *Angolan*.

Anguilla (Formerly St. Christopher-Nevis-Anguilla). *Anguillan*.

Annapolis, Maryland, USA. *Annapolitan*.

Antibes, France. *Antipolitain* or *Antibois*.

Antigua and Barbuda. *Antiguan*.

Antipodes. Term for opposite sides of the Earth. The Antipodes are a group of small uninhabited islands southwest of New Zealand that were so named because they are antipodal to Greenwich, England. A person located on the other side of the Earth from another would be an *antipode* or an *antipodist*. The proper adjective would be *antipodal*, although *antipodean* and *antipodian* are used.
   In his *Good Words to You* the late John Ciardi gave this etymology of the term, which emerged in metaphysical geography when people were still trying to deal with the new concept of a spherical Earth: "Like noses pressed against plate glass at the

same point but from opposite sides, the feet of persons 'down under' were said to oppose those of a person on this side. Gk. *anti*, opposite; *pous*, foot, *podes*, feet."

ANZAC. Name for a resident of Australia or New Zealand. The term originated during World War I when it was an acronym for the Australian-New Zealand Army Corps, the official name for the antipodal unit of the British Army. The heroic 1915 ANZAC landing on the Gallipoli peninsula during the war was commemorated by renaming the landing area ANZAC Cove.

Appalachia, USA (U.S. region comprising the Appalachian Mountains stretching from New York state into Alabama). *Appalachian*. One cannot discuss the connotations carried by this name without mention of the town of Appalachin, N.Y., which was the site of a meeting of 60 underworld figures in November 1957. When the meeting was raided by the police it was big news, and the name took on a special crime connotation. A meeting of underworld figures in 1960 in Buffalo and another in 1965 in Palm Springs, California, and still another in Queens, N.Y., were each immediately dubbed "Little Appalachin." A raid on a teen-age gang meeting in Brooklyn in 1960 was termed "Jr. Appalachin."

Appleknocker/Apple-knocker. Affectionate nickname for people from apple-growing areas such as the orchard-rich counties of upstate New York and Washington state. Bing Crosby, singer and native Washingtonian, was often referred to as one.

   This is an interesting term because it began its life as an insult for a rustic or rube of the laziest type; one who would knock apples off trees instead of picking them. It is now used with a degree of affection rather than disdain.

Aquisextain. Resident of Aix-en-Provence, France; also *Aixois*.

Arabia (Peninsula that includes the nations of Saudi Arabia, both Yemens and the Persian Gulf states). *Arabian*. It is used in the term *Arabian stallion* and the book *The Arabian Nights*. An interesting derivative is *Arabesque,* which is used to describe, among other things, Arabian and Moorish architecture.

Arabian Gulf. Name of the Persian Gulf that the U.S. Department of Defense began using in 1987 despite the fact that the U.S. State Department and other official entities continued using the traditional name. The change was coldly received by all and the *Washington Post* noted that "it's doubtful that it will stick."

Arcadia. *Arcadian.* Arcadia is a mountainous region of ancient Greece, a city in southern California and a real or imagined place of innocence and simplicity.

Argentina (Argentine Republic/Republic of Argentina). *Argentine.* The term *Argentinian* has found its way into print— "The Argentinian sat opposite Daughtry, crossed his long willowy legs and lit a small panatella" (Herbert Lieberman's *Night Call from a Distant Time Zone,* from Charles D. Poe)—but it is less common.

The term *Argie* sometimes appears in print in Britain—"Now it's time to talk to the Argies," headline in the Sunday *London Telegraph,* April 5, 1987—but it appears to be an impolite nickname owing something to the Falklands war.

Arizona (state), **USA.** *Arizonan* is currently preferred, but one finds examples of *Arizonian,* including a 1935 Western movie, *The Arizonian,* starring Richard Dix. William Safire pointed out in his column of June 6, 1982: "Federal style is *Arizonan,* and that is what Senator Barry Goldwater calls himself, but many locals will fight for *Arizonian.*" In a 1947 article for *American Speech,* "Names for Americans," H. L. Mencken noted that *Arizonian* was used by Walt Whitman in one of the early editions of *Leaves of Grass.*

One odd derivative *Arizo-Mex* is used to describe food prepared with a combination of Arizona and Mexican influences.

Traditional nicknames include *Sand Cutter* and *Apache,* a name that was once common but would probably be regarded

with disfavor by American Indians if used today. See also *Zonie*.
COMMON NICKNAME: Grand Canyon State.

Arkansas (state), **USA**. *Arkansawyer*, also *Arkansan* or, more rarely, *Arkansawyan*. In their book *Down in the Holler*, Vance Randolph and George P. Wilson note that the newspapers often use *Arkansan* "but one never hears a hillman pronounce it to rhyme with Kansan." Nevertheless, one finds a *Washington Post* headline proclaiming, "Arkansan Sentenced to Death in 2 Murders" (May 13, 1988).

Randolph and Wilson note that *Arkansawyan* is a compromise between the *-awyer* and *-an* endings. In that spirit, on February 16, 1945, state Senator Julien James introduced a bill designating the people as *Arkansawyans*, but the assembly would have none of it.

The basis for *Arkansawyer* is deeply traditional, following the pronunciation of the state's name. H. L. Mencken reported that the Arkan-*saw* pronunciation became a matter of state law by an act of the legislature approved on March 15, 1881.

Traditional nicknames include *Goober Grabber*, *Josh*, *Toothpick* and *Razorback* (q.v.). See also the separate entry for *Arkie*.
COMMON NICKNAMES: Land of Opportunity. Older nicknames are the Bear State and the Bowie State.

Arkie. Nickname for people from Arkansas, considered derogatory. An Associated Press news item of November 14, 1976 underscores the burden carried by the term. It begins:

> LITTLE ROCK, Ark.—In the past 22 months, Frank White has travelled 142,000 miles around the world promoting Arkansas. His worst problem, he says, isn't the recession or the energy crisis—it's the "Arkie image."

He went on to say that the mention of the name of the state conjured up visions of gun-toting, barefooted hillbillies who shoot outsiders.

See *Okie* for a similarly negative state nickname.

Armenia (Armenian Soviet Socialist Republic, constituent Republic of the Union of Soviet Socialist Republics). *Armenian*.

Asia. *Asian*.
Asiatic is used as both noun and adjective, but it is considered offensive by some Asians. This point was underscored by William and Mary Morris in their *Harper Dictionary of Contemporary Usage*: "When a new form of influenza first swept this country, it was called Asiatic flu. Then it was pointed out that Asians preferred to be called that—*Asians*—rather than *Asiatics*, a term which many regard as derogatory. So the official medical terminology was changed to *Asian flu*." Ironically, Robert W. Chapman noted in his *Adjectives from Proper Names* (1939), "*Asiatic* has virtually displaced *Asian* as *African* displaced *Afric*."

Aspen, Colorado, USA. *Aspenite*. The term tends to show up when excesses are discussed: "One Aspenite named her newborn quarterhorse colt Ted Bundy, saying, 'It'll know how to run'" (Richard W. Larsen, *Bundy: The Deliberate Stranger*).
The term *Aspenization* has come to stand metaphorically for the process by which a place becomes expensive and chic, as this Colorado town has.

Athens, Greece. *Athenian* or *Kerios*.

Atlanta, Georgia, USA. *Atlantan*. The variant *Atlantian*, which once had advocates, is little used today and must be considered without any significant support. In his February 1934 *American Speech* article "Names for Citizens," George R. Stewart, Jr. pointed out that the city's morning newspaper, the *Atlanta Journal*, used the *-ian* form while the evening paper, the *Atlanta Constitution*, used *Atlantan*.

Atlantis. *Atlantan* is the demonym used for the residents of this legendary island continent.

Aturin. Resident of Aire-sur-L'Adour, France.

Auckland, New Zealand. *Aucklander.*

Austin, Texas, USA. *Austinite.*

Australia (Commonwealth of Australia). *Australian.*   The nicknames *Aussie* and *Ozzie* are used broadly and applied in a friendly, nonderogatory manner. The name has a number of derivatives, including *Australiana*, for that which is characteristic of the place; *Australianess*, having Australian qualities; and *Australianism*, for that which is characteristic of Australian English.

Austria (Federal Republic of Austria). *Austrian.*

Avon, England, UK.   *Not* Avon Ladies and Gents, as has been puckishly suggested (in an ad run in Britain for the Computer People), but *Avonian*.

Azerbaijan Soviet Socialist Republic (Constituent Republic of the Union of Soviet Socialist Republics).   *Azerbaijani.* Sometimes the term is spelled *Azerbaidzhani*.
   Research by Charles D. Poe shows that there are two different approaches to the plural short form of this demonym. Some news accounts use the shortened *Azeries* (*USA Today* discussed a feud between "Christian Armenians and Moslem Azeries" [June 24, 1988]), but others use *Azeris* (an Associated Press piece in the *Houston Chronicle* [May 31, 1988] talks of violence between "Armenians and Azeris").

Azores, The. *Azorean.*

B

Babylonia. *Babylonian*.

Baghdad. *Baghdadi*.

Bahama Islands (The Commonwealth of the Bahamas). *Bahamian*.

Bahrain (State of Bahrain). *Bahraini*.

Bajan. Resident of Barbados, also *Barbadian*.

Baltic Nations. (These nations are Estonia, Latvia and Lithuania.) Individuals are usually called by the specific demonym for their country (*Estonian, Latvian or Lithuanian*), but the term *Balt* is often used generally for Baltic nationals. A letter to the *Washington Post* on the subject of the Soviet deportation of "the Balts" said, "The presence of Latvians, Lithuanians and Estonians is so prevalent in the Soviet gulag that the term 'Balt' has become a slang term for all political prisoners." (Letter from Louise McManus, November 21, 1987)

Baltimore, Maryland, USA. *Baltimorean*. Though the *-ean* form shows up without exception, there is evidence that the term *Baltimorian* was used by some in the 19th century. David Shulman found this line in H. B. Fearon's *Sketches of America*

(London, 1818): "...the Baltimorians themselves lay claim to a superior reputation for hospitality, enterprise, and bravery."

Banana-bender. Nickname for a resident of Queensland (state), Australia. Writer and folklorist W. N. Scott, himself a *Queenslander*, discussed a group of Australian state nicknames that he says are mostly used in a derogatory sense, "though not usually as intentional insults." But he points out that it is all a matter of context:

> For instance, two lines of a poem by Graham Jenkin are as follows:
>   "So I grabbed me gear and off I went with a sense of national pride,
>   To show these Yabbies how it's done on the old crow-eating side... "

> Now Jenkin is a South Australian, hence himself a Crow-eater, but his hero's description of the Cabbage-patchers, or Yabbies (which are synonymous) shows that a South Australian does not necessarily object to the description of himself as a Crow-eater. It has become simply a name for an inhabitant of the State of South Australia. Nevertheless, in other circumstances it could be used as an insult if necessary, and great and even violent exception might be taken to the use of the epithet in other circumstances.

Bangkok, Thailand.   No common term is in use; however, this important point is made by librarian Joanne Edwards in the introduction to *Liverpudlian*: "While researching the material, we noted with interest that some regions have no identifying verbal concept of themselves as a unit of people residing together in a specified area. Thus, according to a governmental representative of Thailand, an inhabitant of Bangkok does not identify his place of residence as being that of a city within a country—as say a Londoner might—but rather as a countryman of Thailand, i.e., a Thai."

Bangladesh (People's Republic of Bangladesh).   *Bangladeshi,* according to the CIA's *World Factbook,* which lists the adjective *Bandladesh. Bengalee* is also used as a demonym.

Baraboo, Wisconsin, USA. *Barabooians.* A note from Charles R. Lancaster of Sarasota, Florida reminded us that John Ringling, the circus man, couldn't wait to leave this town, which he cynically said was filled with "hick Baraboobians."

Barbados. *Bajan* or *Barbadian.*

Barbareno. Resident of Santa Barbara, California, although *Santa Barbarans* may be more common.

Barcelona, Spain. *Barcelonians.*

Basotho. Resident of Lesotho.

Baton Rouge, Louisiana, USA. *Baton Rougean.*

Bavaria. *Bavarian,* as in Bavarian cream.

Bay City, Texas, USA. *Bay Cityan.*

Bay Stater. Resident of Massachusetts. For instance, here is the term as it appears in a *Boston Herald* headline for July 18, 1988: "Bay Staters brace for sizzling days." *Bay State* is an adjective for Massachusetts, as in the Bay State Games.

Bean-eater/Beantowner. Traditional, sometimes scornful, nicknames for residents of Boston, Massachusetts. Both derive from the traditional link between Boston and the consumption of baked beans.

Béarn, France. *Béarnais* (male), *Béarnaise* (female). *Béarnaise* is also a culinary term for something prepared in the style of Béarn. A *béarnaise* dish would include shallots, tarragon, local wine and rice.

Beaumont, Texas, USA. *Beaumonter.*

Bedfordshire, England. *Bedfordian.*

Beirut, Lebanon. No common term in use.

Belgian Congo. See **Zaïre.**

Belgium (Kingdom of Belgium). *Belgian.*

Belgravia, London, UK. *Belgravian.*

Belize (Formerly British Honduras). *Belizean.*

Bellifontain. Resident of Fontainebleau, France, along with *Fontainbleen.*

Bender. Resident of South Bend, Indiana.

Benelux. No evidence of a demonym could be found, although if there were one, it would probably be *Beneluxian.* Benelux was a name created from *Bel*gium, the *Ne*therlands and *Lux*embourg to describe the three countries as an ecomonic and cultural entity. The term first came into play in 1947, according to Kenneth Versand's *Polyglot's Lexicon: 1943-1966.*

Bengalee. Resident of Bangladesh.

Benin (People's Republic of Benin, formerly Dahomey). *Beninese* (both singular and plural). This area, controlled by the Beni tribe from the 15th to the mid-17th centuries, was colonized by the French and gained its independence in 1960. It changed its name from Dahomey to Benin in 1975.

Berkeley, California, USA. *Berkeleyite.* The nickname that has been used since the 1960s is *Berserkeleyite* or *Berzerkeley,* which stems from newspaper columnist Herb Caen's coinage "Berserkeley."

Berkshire, England, UK. *Berkshireman/Berkshirewoman.*

Berlin, Germany. *Berliner.* In an article in the winter 1989 issue of *The Spectator,* writer Ken Howard told of President Kennedy's famous speech in which he proclaimed in perfect textbook German, "Ich bin ein Berliner," or "I am a Berliner." Howard points out that some natives thought it funny, "The president and his speechwriters had run afoul of an idiom. 'Ein Berliner' is the local idiom for 'jelly doughnut.'" Reinhold Aman disputes this widely circulated story: "In the context, nobody thought of a doughnut."

Bermuda. *Bermudian*, but sometimes *Bermudan*. *Bermudian* was a very early demonym showing up in a North American newspaper, *The American Weekly Mercury*, as early as 1723.

The nickname *Onion* is sometimes used. It is of course a reference to the Bermuda onion, which has retained its name even though significant numbers of the vegetable have not been exported since the 1930s. The adjective *Bermuda* gets more than its share of attention through Bermuda shorts, Bermuda sailing rig, Bermuda bike, Bermuda Triangle, Bermuda grass, Bermuda cedar, Bermuda petrel and Bermuda collar.

Bern, Switzerland. *Bernese*.

Berry (province), **France**. *Berruyers*. An August 1986 article in *Word Ways* ("*D'où Êtes-Vous* Revisited") notes that residents of the capital of the province, Bourges, are known as *Berrichons*.

Berrichon. See **Berry**.

Berserkeley/Berzerkeley. Nickname for a citizen of Berkeley, California. A seemingly derogatory allusion to the city's eccentricity, it appears to raise few hackles. *Berserkeley* was the name given to a local record label. The following statement appeared in *California Living* (the magazine of the *San Francisco Sunday Examiner and Chronicle*, January 31, 1982): "Berkeley has a certain reputation to uphold. The word Berzerkeley is painted in large black letters along the side of the Cambridge Apartments at Durant and Telegraph. It's been there since I've been here, for three months, so neither city fathers nor street citizens must take particular umbrage."

Bhutan (Kingdom of Bhutan). *Bhutanese* (singular and plural).

Biafra (Breakaway portion of Nigeria that ceased to exist in January 1970). *Biafran.*

Biarritz, France. *Biarrot.*

Birmingham, Alabama, USA. *Birmian.*

Birmingham, England, UK. *Brummie* or *Brum.* It derives from *Brummagem,* an alternative name for the city that Eric Partridge termed "a local vulgar form of Birmingham." *Brummie* has been sanctioned by a number of sources. For instance, in 1966 it appears in a list issued by BOAC, the airline now known as British Airways, of what to call residents of various spots in the British Isles.

Bizonian. Nickname for the people occupying the Anglo-U.S. zone in West Germany immediately following World War II. The area was known as Bizonia (as in bilateral zone).

Bloomington, Illinois and Indiana, USA. *Bloomingtonian.*

Bluenose. Resident of Nova Scotia, Canada; an affectionate name. The province's most famous sailing ship was called the *Blue Nose.*
  In his *Good News to You,* John Ciardi points out that the term took on a separate meaning in the USA in the late 19th century: "A rigorously puritanical person of Spartan habits. (Generally implies moral snooping into the habits of others, and certainly, disaproval of them.)" The notion of the moralistic bluenose was such that it found limited used as a verb: to reform; to kill joy.

Bogotá, Colombia. *Bogotan* or *Bogotano.*

Bohemia (Once a European kingdom now part of Czechoslovakia). *Bohemian.*
  This term has also been applied to artists, writers and others who live outside the realm of conventional standards. Greenwich Village in New York City and the Left Bank of Paris have been known for their Bohemians. This use of the term apparent-

ly stems from the mistaken belief that Bohemia was the European home of the Gypsies. The term *Bohemian* is still sometimes applied to anyone—Gypsy or not—who is seen to have different values than the rest of society.

Bolivia (Republic of Bolivia/Bolivian Republic). *Bolivian*.
The term *Bolivarian* is used to describe something done in the manner of Simon Bolívar. In *Fidel: A Critical Portrait* Tad Szulc talks about a Castro trip to South America as "his first Bolivarian gesture."

Bologna, Italy. *Bolognese*.

Bombay, India. *Bombayite*.

Boondocks/boonies. Generic term. An isolated outpost, the back country. The term, which comes from the Tagalog word *bundok* for mountain, became an English word in the 1920s and gained widespread popularity during World War II for an out-of-the-way place. U.S. marines called their rugged boots—presumably because they were fit for mountain terrain—"boondockers." A collection of citations on the term in the Tamony collection shows it has been applied to a variety of locations, from the suburbs to minor-league baseball towns. It even had a brief slang incarnation as a verb—"to park, to neck"—in the 1950s.
    A number of other alternative meanings exist, including: hick town, whistlestop, sque(e)dunk, jerkwater town, the sticks, a wide spot in the road, East Overshoe, Hicksville, dogpatch, back 40, tank town and *Podunk*, which rates a separate entry.

Bordeaux, France. *Bordelais* (male), *Bordelaise* (female). *Bordelaise* is also a culinary term.

Borinquen. Resident of Puerto Rico, from the name of an Indian tribe on the island at the time of the arrival of Columbus.

Boston, Massachusetts, USA. *Bostonian*. Nicknames dating back into the 19th century include *Bean-eater*, *Bowwow* and

Beantowner. Because the city's longest surviving nickname is "The Hub," Bostonians are often identified as *Hub man* or *Hub woman*. One subspecies of Bostonian is the *Boston Brahmin*. Here is how the term is explained in Francis Russell's *The Great Interlude*:

> It was in reaction to these untouchable newcomers [i.e., the Irish] that the tradition of the Boston *hauteur* came into being, the proper Bostonian, the myth of the Brahmin—that term kindly Dr. Oliver Wendell Holmes coined originally to mean no more than a bread-and-water intellectual asceticism and that would now come to mean a class-conscious membership in the Yankee State Street financial oligarchy.

See also ***Proper Bostonian***.

Boswash/Bosnywash. Name made popular in the 1960s by futurists for the immense city that would someday stretch from Boston to Washington. *Boswasher.*

Botswana (Republic of Botswana, formerly British Protectorate of Bechuanaland). *Motswana in the singular, but Botswana* in the plural, according to the CIA's *World Factbook. Botswani* is also used. The common adjective used by the press is *Botswanan*.

Bourges, France. Capital of the department of Cher (the former province of Berry). *Berrichons.*

Bowery, New York City, USA, The. *Boweryite.*

Bragard. Resident of Saint-Dizier, France.

Brahmin. See **Boston**.

Brazil (Federative Republic of Brazil, but the United States of Brazil prior to 1967). *Brazilian.* The same word is used for the adjective but not in the specific case of the Brazil nut.

Bridgeport, Connecticut, USA. *Bridgeporter.*

Bristol, England, UK. *Bristolian.*

Brit. Slangy nickname for Britain that can be used for people or as an adjective—"Brit culture runs the gamut" (headline in the *Bangor Daily News* travel section, July 18, 1987). The term is not usually derogatory and points to a conclusion made by N. Sally Hass: "It's hard to tell just what makes a shortened demonym insulting. 'Jap' for Japanese is highly offensive, but 'Brit' for Briton is not. The British use it themselves."

Britain. Short for Great Britain, which consists of England, Scotland and Wales. A resident of Britain is a *Briton*.

Britannic. Rare adjective for Great Britain. Robert W. Chapman addressed the word in his *Adjectives from Proper Names* (1939): "It is now hardly used except in the formal 'His Britannic Majesty' and as the name of a ship." There is also the world-famous *Encyclopedia Britannica*.

British. The collective plural (*Briton* is the singular) and the adjective for Great Britain, consisting of England, Scotland and Wales. It is used in many terms and proper names, including the British Broadcasting Corp. (BBC) and British thermal unit (BTU).

British Columbia (province), **Canada**. *British Columbian*.

Britisher. Resident of Great Britain, but *Briton* is preferred by the British.
  This is an informal term that, according to several sources, became popular in the United States during and immediately after the Revolution and was meant to be derogatory. One theory holds that the term was used as means of distinguishing a British army of occupation from the English-born colonists.
  Today it seems to be used ironically as a playful poke at overblown, stuffy titles. In Alistair MacLean's thriller *Ice Station Zebra* an American character calls an English character a Britisher as a friendly tweak. The Briton later talks of "decadent Britishers."

British Honduras. *British Honduran*, now obsolete; see *Belize*.

British Virgin Islands. *Virgin Islander.*

Briton. Resident of Great Britain.

Brobdingnagian. Giant from a land of giants in Jonathan Swift's *Gulliver's Travels*. Used for anything that is tremendous in size.

Bronx, New York, New York, USA. *Bronxite.*
   Adjective: Bronx. New Yorkers always refer to this borough as "The Bronx." (William Safire says that the classic apocryphal question from the carpetbagging politician is, "Where are the Bronx?") Sometimes used in rough and tumble characterizations on the order of Bronx bagpipe, a vacuum cleaner, and the internationally known Bronx cheer, for a flatulent razz.

Brooklyn, New York, New York, USA. *Brooklynite.*

Brooklynese. An accent and manner of speaking that can be heard from New Jersey to the middle of Long Island, but which has always been most closely associated with Brooklyn. It is characterized by t's that become d's (boddle of Bud,) dropped g's and r's (talkin' to my fatha') and a disregard for the th sound (toidy-toid for 33rd). Charles F. Dery recalls the illustrative anecdote involving the Brooklyn-born Hall-of-Famer Waite Hoyt, who in 1938, the last of his 21 seasons as a major leaguer, pitched for Brooklyn. "As you will no doubt recall," Dery wrote to Peter Tamony, "when Hoyt was injured an anonymous Brooklyn cried out: 'Hert is hoit!'"

Brum or *Brummie.* Resident of Birmingham, England.

Brunei (State of Brunei Darussalam). *Bruneian.*

Brussels, Belgium. *Bruxellois* (French). In *Liverpudlian*, Joanne Edwards points out: "An inhabitant of Brussels has no Flemish term to describe himself as a resident of that city. He does, however, use the French term Bruxellois to indicate the same."
   The name of the vegetable is brussels sprouts.

Bruxellois/Bruxelloise. French for resident (male, female) of Brussels, Belgium.

Buckinghamshire, England, UK. *Bucksian.*

Budapest, Hungary. *Budapestiek* is often found in print but the informal *Pesti* is common. "A Pesti (pronounced Peshtee) as the local citizens are called," says an April 4, 1989 report in the *Wall Street Journal*, "is a person who believes only half or what he/she sees, then puts that half under a microscope to see in whose interest it is to appear that way."

Buenos Aires, Argentina. *Porteño* (male) and *Porteña* (female).

Buffalo, New York, USA. *Buffalonian*, not Buffaloan.

Bulgaria (People's Republic of Bulgaria). *Bulgarian.*

Bunnies. Playful "gag" name for a resident of Cedar Rapids, Iowa, a play on "See Der Rabbits." It is one of a number of tongue-in-cheek or insulting forms: Mencken listed *Chicagorilla, Baltimorons, Omahogs* and *Louisvillains.* There have also been *Hollywoodenheads* and *Madhattaners.* A man from Santa Barbara notes that the facetious *Santa Barbarian* and *Stabarbarans* are used locally. Lexicographer David Shulman has dubbed a loud-mouth from Illinois an *Illinoisy.*

At another level, some make a game of coming up with lists of punning or whimsical demonyms. For instance, John Masengrab published a list of these in the *Minneapolis/St. Paul Magazine* based on local towns like Blue Earth (populated by *Blue Earthlings*), Esko (*Eskimoes*) and Proctor (*Proctologists*). Several collections have appeared in *Word Ways*, including one by Vernon Maclaren ("How to Name the Residents," May 1988) that included names for people from Holyoke (*Holyokels*), Armonk (*Armonkeys*), Saratoga (*Saratogres*) and Waterloo (*Waterloonies*).

Such local wordplay can be quite clever. A note from Emily Harrison Wier of Northampton, Massachusetts reports: "Resi-

dents of Burlington, Vermont, are called—quite predictably—
Burlingtonians. But supporters of Burlington's socialist Mayor
Bernard Sanders are referred to—quite ingeniously I think—as
'*Sanderistas*.'" A few contain a modicum or more of hostility, as
displayed in this line from Johnny France and Malcolm
McConnell's *Incident at Big Sky*: "That was Resort Montana, an
all-season recreational preserve for wealthy Easterners and the
tanned Calvin Klein set some of the old ranchers called *Califor-
nicators*.'" Reinhold Aman has coined Waukeshite for anti-in-
tellectual locals in his community of Waukesha, Wisconsin.
   See also *Maineiac*.

Burgundy, France. *Burgundian*.

Burkina Faso (Formerly Upper Volta; the name was changed
in 1984). *Burkinabé*. The nation is often referred to as Burkina
for short.
   Adjective: *Burkinabé*, although *Burkinian* appears in some
news reports.

Burlington, Vermont, USA. *Burlingtonian*.

Burma (Socialist Republic of the Union of Burma). *Burmese*,
but the name of the country was changed to Myanma in early
1989 making the Burmese *Myanmen*. *Burmese* is still used to
describe members of the nation's ethnic majority, the Burmese.

Burundi (Republic of Burundi, formerly the Belgian trus-
teeship territory of Ruanda-Urundi). *Burundian*. Adjective:
Burundi.

Byelorussian Soviet Socialist Republic (Constituent Republic of the Union of Soviet Socialist Republics). *Byelorussian*.

Byetowner. Resident of Ottawa, Canada; *Ottawan*. Canadian
onomastician Jay Ames explains, "'Ottawan' is obvious
enough, but 'Byetowner' less so unless you happen to know
that the settlement was named for British Army Engineer
Colonel William Bye. He and his men built the Rideau Canal
and the Trent water systems of canals and locks."

C

Cabbage-patcher. Resident of Victoria (state), Australia. See entry for *Banana-Bender*.

Cairo, Egypt. *Cairoen* or *Cairene*. "Spring is a glorious season here," read a recent dispatch from Cairo in the *New York Times*, "Cairenes take to the parks and streets."

Cajun. Louisianian of Acadian-French descent; a slurring corruption of *Acadian* in the same manner that "injun" was taken from *Indian*. Acadia was the French colony formed at the Bay of Fundy in 1604 and whose residents were expelled by the British Crown in 1755. About one in four residents of Louisiana calls him- or herself a *Cajun*. Used in references to food (Cajun cooking), music and one early U.S. guided missile (the Nike-Cajun).

Calabria, Italy. *Calabrian* or *Calabrese*.

Calcutta, India. *Calcuttan*.

Caledonian. Scot (n.) or Scottish (adj.), this ancient term means "men of the woods" or "men of the thistle."

Calgary, Alberta, Canada. *Calgarian*. Traditional personal nicknames: *Cowtowners* and *Stampeders*.

California (state), **USA**. *Californian*. The term *Californios* is reserved for the area's early Spanish-speaking inhabitants (as in the title of the book *The Decline of the Californios: A History of Spanish-Speaking Californians 1846-1890* by Leonard Pitt, University of California Press, 1966).

Among the derivatives, *Californianize* or *Californiazation*: to be dominated by or to become like California. An article on the growing congressional delegation from California in the March 27, 1988 *Roll Call* was entitled "The Californiazation of Congress." A crude but popular synonym is *Californicate*, as printed on a series of Western bumper stickers that first appeared in the late 1970s: DON'T CALIFORNICATE MONTANA, DON'T CALIFORNICATE OREGON, etc. Many of these derivatives rely on a stereotype (reinforced by advertising) of a land of beans sprouters, bikinis and blondes.

Traditional nicknames include *Gold Coaster*, *Gold Digger* and *Prune Picker*.

COMMON NICKNAMES: The Golden State and El Dorado.

Cambodia. *Cambodian*. Kampuchea was the official name of the country until early 1989 but Cambodia and *Cambodian* still held the upper hand in English during that period. For instance, the *AP Stylebook* (1980) said, "Use this name [Cambodia] rather than *Democratic Kampuchea* in datelines. When *Kampuchea* is used in the body of a story, it should be identified as the formal name of Cambodia."

Cambridge, England, UK. *Cantabridgian*. This is customary for both residents of the English municipality and graduates of Cambridge University. *Cantab* is used colloquially.

Cambridge, Massachusetts, USA. *Cantabridgian*. This term is often shortened to *Cantab* in newspapers. Both the long and short form are sometimes applied to students and graduates of Harvard University, located in Cambridge.

Camden, New Jersey, USA. *Camdenite*.

Cameroon (United Republic of Cameroon). *Cameroonian.* Cameroon is sometimes spelled Camerouns or Cameroun but neither is found in recent U.S. usage.

Canada. *Canadian.*

An illuminating note appears in *Columbo's Canadian References* under the entry on "Canadian": "Before the passage of the Canadian Citizenship Act which came into force on 1 Jan. 1947, a Canadian could not call himself or herself a Canadian citizen because the official designation for a person born or naturalized within the British Commonwealth was British Subject. The Act created the distinct nationality of a Canadian citizen… "

In his *Adjectives from Proper Names* (1939), Robert W. Chapman comments on this term: "I am not clear why *Canadan* was avoided, but *Canadian* is no doubt French." Although *Canadian* is the preferred adjective, there are a few exceptions such as "Canada goose."

Canal Zone, Panama. *Zonian* is what Americans in the area are called.

Cantabridgian. Resident of Cambridge, Massachusetts, USA, as well as those associated with Harvard University.

Cantabrigian. Resident of Cambridge, England, or a graduate of Cambridge University.

Canton, Ohio, USA. *Cantonian.*

Canton, People's Republic of China. *Cantonese.*

Canuck. A Canadian, in early use, specifically, a French-Canadian.

This is a difficult term to typify because it is clearly derogatory and offensive in some cases but not so in others. In eastern Canada and northern New England it is seen as a racial slur by French-Canadians. In western Canada it is used, among other things, as a nickname for a hockey team: the Vancouver

Canucks. John Ciardi in his 1987 book *Good Words to You* terms it "once pejorative, now commonly accepted by Canadians as a fond nickname." Ciardi does acknowledge that it became "more-or-less pejorative" for French-Canadian in northern New England. In this regard, Senator Edmund Muskie was accused in a published letter of laughing at the use of the term during his 1972 presidential campaign. He denied the charge and the letter was seen as probably spurious, but it focused attention on the term and left little doubt that it was considered a slur in the northeastern United States.

The Associated Press Stylebook and Libel Manual is less tolerant of the term's use. It calls it a "derogatory racial label" and cautions its writers, "Avoid the word except in formal names (The Vancouver Canucks...) or in quoted matter."

Canadian Phillip Chaplin has summarized his attempts to track the etymology of the term: "The *Oxford English Dictionary (supplement)* says apparently from the first syllable of Canada, *Encyclopedia Canadiana* gives that, with an Algonkian ending -*uc* as one possibility, *Appleton-Century* says 'N. Amer. Ind.', and Vinay [*Dictionaire Canadien*] ignores the word. *Canadiana* seems to prefer to trace it to a French attempt at Connaught, originally applying to Irish immigrants, but then says it was used first of French-Canadians. *Oxford English Dictionary's* earliest quotation is dated 1855, but *Canadiana* gives one from the Boston *Transcript* of 1840, and claims the word was in use in 1835."

Cape Cod, Massachusetts, USA. *Cape Codder*. See also *Washashore*.

Cape Town, South Africa. *Capetonian*.

Cape Verde (Republic of Cape Verde). *Cape Verian*; however, the CIA's *World Factbook* says *Cape Verdean*.

Caracas, Venezuela. *Caraqueño* (male) or *Caraqueña* (female).

Carioca. Resident of Rio de Janeiro, Brazil. In the novel *Isle of the Snakes* by Robert L. Fish, a character asks, "Were they from Rio, do you think? Cariocas?"

Carolinian. Resident of North or South Carolina.

Carolopolitain. Resident of Charlesville, France.

Carpinien/Carpinienne. Resident of Charmes, France.

Cedar Rapids, Iowa, USA. *Cedar Rapidian.* There is also the joking term *Bunnies* (*q.v.*), a pun based on "See Der Rabbits."

Celt/Celtic. Person from the Celtic lands, which include Ireland, Highland Scotland, Wales and Cornwall.

Central African Republic (Former French colony of Ubanghi Shari). *Central African.*

Cestrian. Resident of Chester or Cheshire, England.

Ceylon. *Ceylonese,* obsolete: now Sri Lanka. *The Associated Press Stylebook and Libel Manual* notes that "the people [of Sri Lanka] may be referred to as *Ceylonese* (n. or adj.) or *Sri Lankans.*"

Chad (Republic of Chad, formerly part of French Equatorial Africa). *Chadian.*

Chamorro. See **Guam.**

Channel Islands. *Channel Islander,* although a resident is commonly addressed for the specific island, such as *Jerseyan, Jerseyite* or *Jerseyman/Jerseywoman* for the Isle of Jersey.

Charleston, West Virginia, and Charleston, North Carolina, USA. *Charlestoner.*

Charlestown (Part of Boston, Massachusetts, USA). *Charlestoner.*

Charlestown, West Virginia, USA. *Charles Towner.*

Charlesville, France. *Carolopolitain*.

Charlotte, North Carolina, USA. *Charlottean*.

Charlottetown, Prince Edward Island, Canada. *Charlotte-towner*.

Charmes, France. *Carpinien* (male) or *Carpinienne* (female).

Chaseburg, Wisconsin, USA. *Chaseburger*. By the way, Chaseburg is in Hamburg Township. This was verified some years ago by Bill Gold of the *Washington Post*, who went on to ask, "Is Champ, Md. peopled by 'Champions' and Childs, Md. by 'Children'?"

Chatauqua, New York, USA. *Chatauquan*.
  Term has wider use because an adult education movement started in the town in 1874 and grew into a national movement. Engaged in religious and secular studies as well as the performing arts, local chapters became known as Chautauquas and those involved were known as *Chatauquans*.

Chattanooga, Tennessee, USA. *Chattanoogan*.

Cheshire, England, UK. *Cestrian*. Traditional personal nickname *Cat*, from "Cheshire Cat."

Chester, England, UK. *Cestrian*.

Chicago, Illinois, USA. *Chicagoan*. Never *Chicagan*. It is occasionally argued that *Chicagan* would be consistent with demonyms like *San Franciscan* and *Coloradan*, but the counterargument is that these other names are Spanish while Chicago is of Indian origin.
  Adjective: *Chicago*. It has been used in a number of hurly-burly slang constructions, including *Chicago majority* (105% of the vote), *Chicago piano* (a machine gun) and *Chicago rubdown* (a thrashing).
  One who works in Chicago's famous Loop is known as a *Looper*, an example how these geographical nouns can work down to the neighborhood level.

Chicano. An American of Mexican descent, in current use this term seems to be preferred over Mexican-American by some. The 1980 *Associated Press Stylebook and Libel Manual*, however, advises that it should not be used for routine description of Mexican-Americans. It adds, "*Chicano* has been adopted by some social activists of Mexican descent, and may be used when activists use it to describe themselves. To apply it to all Spanish-surnamed citizens would be roughly the same as calling all blacks Muslims."

Chichester, England, UK. *Cisestrian.*

Chilango. Resident of Mexico City. An example in print: "But the first weeks of the year are always a particular trial for chilangos, as natives of the Mexican capital are known, because of the regularity and severity of atmospheric inversions." (*New York Times*, January 16, 1988)

Chile (Republic of Chile). *Chilean.* Before World War I Chile was often spelled *Chili*, which made residents *Chilian.*

China (People's Republic of China). *Chinese* (both singular and plural). *Chinaman/Chinawoman* has become increasingly scarce, because it is widely regarded as a term of condescension and derision. "A patronizing term" says *The Associated Press Stylebook and Libel Manual*, which advises its writers to confine its use to quoted matter. The slang *Chinee* is unquestionably derogatory as it was often used in the 19th-century notion of "heathen Chinee."

One of the reasons why *Chinaman* is viewed as a slur has been its long and varied history in slang. Variously, a *chinaman* is or has been an illegible figure on a racetrack tote board; to have a chinaman on one's back means to be addicted and is a synonym for a monkey on one's back; and a "chinaman's chance" is no chance. The personification "John Chinaman," which was used for all Chinese, no doubt contributed because the name was an expression of the idea that all Chinese were alike and without individual identity. The degree to which the term is seen to be derogatory is shown in two newspaper clippings from the *San*

Francisco Sunday Examiner and Chronicle in the Tamony Collection. The first is about a man who was referred to as a Chinaman by an official of the sheriff's office and is headlined "Sheriff probes racial slur on Chinese man" (August, 26, 1979), and the second is this from Herb Caen's column: "Nobody asked me, but why is it that the words Frenchman and Englishman are not offensive but the word Chinaman is? And it is. Ask any Chinese." (August, 1, 1971)

China (Republic of China).   See **Taiwan**.

Chinatown.   Name for any of a number of Chinese districts in major cities in which large numbers of Chinese have settled. The term *Chinatowner* was given a meaning in the New York garment industry, which has nothing to do with Chinatowns east or west. It refers to the manufacturers of cheap dresses and probably derives from the fact that they once paid their workers "coolie wages."

Cincinnati, Ohio, USA.   *Cincinnatian*. Residents of the Queen City have also been called *Porkopolitans* and *Rhinelanders* (*q.v.*), but these terms are not commonly used today.

citizen.   Generic term. A person who has achieved the full civil rights of a nation by birth or naturalization.
   The Associated Press Stylebook and Libel Manual points out that cities and states do not confer citizenship. Therefore it suggests, "To avoid confusion, use *resident*, not *citizen*, in referring to inhabitants of states and cities."

Cleveland, Ohio, USA.   *Clevelander*.

Clodoaldien/Clodoaldienne.   Resident of Saint-Cloud, France.

Collioure, France.   *Colliourench*, according to *"D'où Êtes-Vous Revisited,"* (Word Wurcher, *Word Ways*, August 1986).

Colorado (state), **USA**.   *Coloradan*. The variant *Coloradoan* shows up in print with some regularity, but it is unpopular with natives of the state. In keeping with the practice of dropping the *-o* when creating a demonym from a Spanish name (Colorado is Spanish for "colored"), the case for *Coloradan* becomes stronger.

Traditional nicknames include *Centennial, Rover* and *Silverine*. *COMMON NICKNAMES*: Centennial State, because it was admitted to the Union in 1876, America's Centennial year.

Colombia (Republic of Colombia). *Colombian*. This is the only New World nation named for Christopher Columbus.

The term *Columbian* is also used to describe something or someone that relates to Christopher Columbus (such as the Columbian Exposition of 1893).

Colombo, Ceylon. No common term appears to be in use.

Columbus, Georgia, Indiana, Nebraska and Ohio, USA. *Columbusite.*

Columbus, Mississippi, USA. *Columbian.*

Commonwealth (Formerly the British Commonwealth). No common term exists. The Commonwealth is a free association of sovereign states that recognize the British sovereign as head of the Commonwealth.

Comoros (Federal Islamic Republic of the Comoros). *Comoran.*

Congo (People's Republic of the Congo). *Congolese.* Adjective: *Congolese* or *Congo*, as in Congo River. (The Congo River is commonly accepted; however, it is called the Zaïre by people on that bank of the river.)

Connecticut (state), **USA**. *Nutmegger*. The adjective *Nutmegian* is seldom used.

There is no hint of derogation in *Nutmegger* despite the fact that it refers to Yankee skulduggery. The demonym takes its name from the long-established state nickname, the Nutmeg

State. The reference to nutmegs was spelled out by William F. Buckley, Jr. in the *National Review* (September 16, 1988): "Connecticut traders went out in the seventeenth and eighteenth centuries to sell nutmeg. But when they ran out of the real stuff, they sold sawdust instead, and called it nutmeg; and everyone thought this absolutely hilarious, and Connecticut celebrated its miscreants by nicknaming itself after the symbol of their misdeeds."

A proper demonym for the state has been a matter of long-standing debate and deliberation. For decades the public printer of the United States has used *Connecticuter* in publications created by the Government Printing Office (GPO), but this has been widely ignored and derided outside government ("...a display of Federal arrogance..." is how William Safire typified it in his column of June 6, 1982).

Columbia University Professor Allen Walker Read (who has gone on the record opposing the GPO's *Connecticuter* with one *t*) once researched this topic and found an impressive list of early attempts:

Connecticotian (Cotton Mather, 1702), *Connecticutensian* (Samuel Peters, 1781), and *Connecticutter* (a California periodical, *Land of Sunshine*, 1897).

After these came *Connectican* (1942), *Connecticutan* (1946), *Connecticutian* (1947) and *Connecticutite* (1968). In addition to these serious suggestions Read found six jocular alternatives: *Quonaughicotter* (from H.L. Mencken), *Connecticutey, Connecticanuck, Connectikook* (from Read himself), *Connectecotton* and *Connecticutist*.

J. Baxter Newgate, a writer known for his skillful wordplay, suggested *Connecticutlet*. A letter to the editor of the *Willimantic Journal* (May 20, 1988) from Babs Johnson suggests a blend of Connecticut + Yankee = *Connecticutee*.

The suggestion *Connecticutup* is made in the May 1988 issue of *Word Ways*. Allan D. Pratt of New Haven, with an eye to the parkways and train lines, has pointed out that "...by far the most common term used to describe residents of Connecticut is 'Commuters.'"

Traditional personal nicknames include *Nutmeg* or *Wooden Nutmeg*.

COMMON NICKNAMES: Nutmeg State and Constitution State.

Cook Islands. *Cook Islander.*

Copenhagen, Denmark. *Copenhagener.*

Cork, Ireland. *Corkonian* or *Corkagian.*

Cornhusker. Resident of Nebraska, although *Nebraskan* is allowed.

Cornstalk. Resident of New South Wales (state), Australia. See entry for **Banana-Bender.**

Cornwall, England, UK. *Cornishman/Cornishwoman.* Adjective: *Cornish* as in Cornish game hen. Jay Ames, who has collected many demonyms, has spotted examples of *Cornwallian* and *Cornwellian.* A common nickname for Cornish individuals is either *Cousin Jack* or *Cousin Jenny.*

Corpus Christi, Texas, USA. *Corpus Christians,* regardless of their religious affiliation.

Corsica, France. *Corsican.*

Costa Rica (Republic of Costa Rica). *Costa Rican.* Less common than it was once, it has been written as one word, *Costarican.*

countian. Generic term. Used in giving a name to a county resident when a specific name does not exist or is too cumbersome. A headline in the *Chronicle* of Montgomery County, Maryland, on an expected comet read: "Countians to see Halley's light show" (October 16, 1985).

Cracker. Southern U.S. backwoodsman, especially one residing in Georgia and Florida. Like so many slang terms of its type, this one can be regarded as a slur or affectionate label depending on its context. A 1988 notice from the Largo (Florida) Historical Society announces the 14th annual Cracker Supper, at which traditional backwoods food is served and newcomers are inducted as honorary Crackers. However, after the popular comic strip "Bloom County" used the term in jest in 1985, the *Washington Post* carried a letter from a man terming the word an "ethnic slur" and "a demeaning and insensitive insult to a large and virtually defenseless group of Americans" (June 4, 1985).

Crete (Island of Crete). *Cretan.*

Crow-eater. Resident of South Australia (state), Australia. See entry for **Banana-Bender**, in which the sometimes derogatory nature of this term is discussed.

Cruzan. Resident of St. Croix, Virgin Islands.

Cuba (Republic of Cuba). *Cuban.*

Cumberland, England, UK. People from the area of this former county are known as *Cumberlanders* or *Cumbrians*, after the current name Cumbria, which encompasses both the old Cumberland and Westmorland counties.

Cyprus (Republic of Cyprus). *Cypriot.*   The   alternative *Cypriote* is acceptable but seldom used.

Cytherean. The adjective now generally used to describe the planet Venus and its hypothetical inhabitants.

Czechoslovakia (Czechoslovak Socialist Republic).   *Czechoslovak* for the population as a whole, but *Czech* is used for those in the Czech lands (Bohemia and Moravia-Silesia) and *Slovak* for those in Slovakia.

D

Dahomey (Republic of Dahomey). *Dahomeyan, Dahoman* or *Dahomean*. All are obsolete because the country is now called Benin. See **Benin**.

Dakotan. Resident of North or South Dakota. See *North Dakotan*.

Dallas, Texas, USA. *Dallasite*.

Danube. Residents along the European river are called *Danubians*.

Danzig. (German for Gdansk, Poland. The territory surrounding and including Gdansk that was a free city between the two world wars.) Danziger.

Dayton, Ohio, USA. *Daytonian*.

Daytona Beach, Florida, USA. *Daytonan*.

Dearborn, Michigan, USA. *Dearbornite*.

Delaware (state), **USA**. *Delawarean*.

COMMON NICKNAMES: First State, Diamond State (in that it is small and precious) and the Blue Hen State—from the fact that a Revolutionary War commander liked to bet on cockfights in which he favored the "blue hen's" chickens. The brigade was soon called the Blue Hen Brigade and the name later was adopted as a state nickname).

Delhite. Resident of New Delhi, India.

Del Mar, California, USA. *Del Martian* (jocular but used). See entry for **Ocean Beach**.

Denmark (Kingdom of Denmark). *Dane*. Adjective: *Danish* as in Danish pastry or Danish modern.

Denver, Colorado, USA. *Denverite*. A common commercial Denver adjective in this the "Mile-High City" is Mile-High. There are, according to one report, famous examples like Mile-High Stadium, and "enough other Mile-High (or -Hi) shops, parks, schools and churches to fill four columns of the Denver telephone directory" (*Washington Post*, May 28, 1985).

Déodatien. Male resident of Saint-Dié, France. Female resident is *Déodatienne*.

Derbyshire (county), **England, UK**. *Darbyite* or *Darbian*.

Des Moines, Iowa, USA. *Des Moinesite*.

Detroit, Michigan, USA. *Detroiter*.
  The language of the American automobile trade has been called *Detroitese* and many references to the city (i.e., "Detroit's thinking on imports") allude to the automotive industry rather than the actual city.

Devonshire (county), **England, UK**. *Devonian* or *Devonite*.

Dijon, France. *Dijonese*.

District of Columbia, USA. *Washingtonian*, not Columbian, although one of the common suggestions for the name of the district—should it become the 51st state—is New Columbia.

Dixie/Dixieland. Nickname for the U.S. South. The demonym *Dixieite* has been cited in M. M. Mathews', *Dictionary of American English*, but it is rare and the term *Southerner* is almost always used. The opposite is true for the North, where *Yankee* is common for a Northerner but the region is seldom called Yankeedom. As an adjective it shows up as a pure synonym for Southern (as in "Dixie Mafia" for Southern gangsters) and in compounds such as *Dixiecrat*, the name for the rebellious anti-Truman Southern Democrats of 1948.

Djakarta, Indonesia. *Djakartan*.

Djibouti (Republic of Djibouti, formerly French Territory of the Afars and Issas). *Djibouti*.

Dodge City, Kansas, USA. *Dodge Citian*.

Dominica (Commonwealth of Dominica). Residents of this small island-nation in the West Indies share the name *Dominican* with residents of the Dominican Republic and members of the Roman Catholic order founded by Saint Dominic.

Dominican Republic. *Dominican*.

Dorpian. Resident of Schenectady, New York, an alternative to *Schenectadian*. See entry for **Schenectady**.

Down Easter. One from Down East, the realm from Boston to the tip of Maine. It is usually applied to Mainers and is so common there that the magazine devoted to the state is called *Down East*. In fact, *The Associated Press Stylebook and Libel Manual* stipulates that it only be used in reference to Maine; the terms *Down East* and *Down Easter* are not used for anything or anyone not from Maine as they imply a certain traditionalism and local color.

Several theories have been advanced on the origin of the term. This one appears in a display of Down East schooners at the Penobscot Marine Museum in Searsport, Maine:

> Down East, a nautical term which can be traced to the 1800s. Coastal schooners sailed from Boston to Maine setting their course northeast. They sailed with the prevailing southwest wind or downwind; hence, the term Down East. Down Easter [is a] person or vessel hailing from that region.

A second theory, which is described in William and Mary Morris' *Harper Dictionary of Contemporary Usage*, is that it started as a carryover of a British speech pattern in which anyone going to London is going up to London and anyone leaving is going down to wherever it is that he or she is going. This use of up and down obtains regardless of the direction that one is coming from or going to. The Morrises suggest that this was applied to early Boston—the self-described Hub of the Universe—and that to head out of town was to go down east or down to Maine.

Down Under. Nickname for Australia and New Zealand together.

Dubai (One of the United Arab Emirates). *Emirian.*

Dublin, Ireland. *Dubliner.*

Duluth, Minnesota, USA. *Duluthian.*

Dundee, Scotland, UK. *Dundonian.*

Dun-le-Palleteau, Dun-sur-Aurons and Dun-sur-Meuse, France. Three towns that according to *"D'où Êtes-Vous Revisited"* (*Word Ways*, August 1986) have separate demonyms: people from Dun-le-Palleteau and Dun-sur-Aurons are *Dunois* while those from Dun-sur-Meuse are *Duniens*.

Dunelmain. Resident of Durham City, England.

Durban, South Africa. *Durbanite*.

Durham City, England, UK. *Dunelmain*.

Düsseldorf, Germany. *Düsseldorfer*.

Dutch. Adjective used for the Netherlands. Corresponding name of a resident is *Dutchman/Dutchwoman*. The term has many legitimate uses; however, it has a long history as an adjective of derogation. All evidence points to the origin of this negative use of Dutch coming from the British Isles and then moving to the United States. Why the good people of the Netherlands have been made to suffer so in English calls for some explanation. By all accounts, the pejorative use of the name Dutch dates back to the 17th century when the British and the Dutch fought over control of the sea and parts of the New World. Not only did the British start the tradition of hostile Dutch slurs but actually wiped out Dutch names when territory changed hands. New Amsterdam became New York as soon as the British took over in 1664. In *The American Language: Supplement I*, H.L. Mencken traces the English use of the derisive Dutch back to 1608, but adds that many of the slurs started in the United States, where some may have been aimed at Germans, who have been called "Dutch" for generations. This came about as German immigrants referred to themselves as *Deutsch*, German for German. Those with the nickname Dutch were, in fact, seldom from the Netherlands but of German background. For this reason, many a Dutch immigrant referred to himself as a Hollander or Netherlander.

One Dutch term, "Dutch courage," appears to have come from an actual facet of Dutch life rather than from a generalized dislike. In their *Naval Terms Dictionary* John V. Noel and Edward L. Beach give it this definition: "The courage obtained from drink. Comes from the custom initiated by the famous Dutch Admirals, Tromp and de Ruyter, of giving their crews a liberal libation before battle with the English. The practice was naturally belittled by the English, who nevertheless were forced to admit the effectiveness of the Dutch Navy."

After consulting slang dictionaries dating back to 1811 and a number of specialized dictionaries, it became apparent how pervasive the Dutch slur became and continues to be.

double Dutch—gibberish, also a jump rope term for jumping with two ropes

Dutch act—suicide

Dutch auction—one that starts with a high bid and works down

Dutch bargain—a one-sided deal, not a bargain at all

Dutch barn—a barn without sides

Dutch bath—an acid bath used in etching

Dutch book—a bookmaker's account book

Dutch brig—a cell in which punishment is meted out

Dutch build—a squat person

Dutch cap—a condom

Dutch cheese—baldness

Dutch clock—a bedpan

Dutch comfort—consolation typified by the line, "It could have been worse" (also known as Dutch consolation)

Dutch concert—a concert in which everyone plays a different tune, or sings a different song (also known as a Dutch medley)

Dutch courage—bravery inspired by drinking

Dutch daub—a mediocre painting, ironic since there were so many great Dutch painters

Dutch defense—surrender, no defense at all

Dutch drink—emptying a glass in one gulp

Dutch elm disease—not the same kind of slur as the others, but it goes to show how unlucky the Dutch are when it comes to naming

Dutch feast—a dinner at which the host gets drunk before the guests do, or worse yet one where the host is drunk before the guests arrive

Dutch fit—a fit of rage

Dutch gleek—liquor

Dutch leave—to be AWOL, a term that became popular during the Spanish-American War

Dutch nightingale—a frog

Dutch oven—a deep iron skillet with legs and a lid

Dutch palate—coarse taste

Dutch pink—boxer's term for blood

Dutch pump—sailor's punishment in which he is thrown overboard and must tread water, or pump, to keep from drowning

Dutch reckoning—guesswork, or a disputed bill

Dutch rod—a Luger pistol

Dutch row—a faked altercation

Dutch roll—aviation, combined yaw and roll in an aircraft and something to be avoided as if can cause a plane to go out of control (proof that some of these Dutch slurs are new because the earliest reference to be found is in a 1950 issue of *Popular Science*)

Dutch route—suicide

Dutch rub—an intense painful rubbing with the knuckles, usually to the scalp

Dutch silver—a silver plate

Dutch steak—hamburger

Dutch tilt—a television and movie term for a camera that has been tilted from the horizontal for dramatic effect

Dutch treat—a treat whose price is shared by host and guest(s)

Dutch uncle—a severe, disciplinary man

Dutch wheelbarrow—taking someone by their legs as they walk with their hands

Dutch widow—a prostitute

Dutch wife (or Dutch husband)—a feather pillow, or a poor bed companion, or, more recently, an inflatable rubber sex partner

Dutchifying—converting a ship's square-stern into a round stern; frequently done to men-of-war in the early 19th century

Dutchman—a piece of wood or stone used to fill a hollow space

Dutchman's headache—drunkenness

Dutchman's anchor—anything left at home, from the tale of a Dutch sea captain who explained after he had lost his ship, that he had a good anchor but had left it at home

Dutchman's breeches—a small blue patch in the sky

Dutchman's cape—imaginary land

Dutchman's drink—a draught that empties the vessel

Dutchy—slovenly

In addition there are Dutch phrases.

as drunk as a Dutchman

Well, I'll be a Dutchman's uncle—an expression of surprise

It beats the Dutch—applied to anything that is monstrous, startling or inexplicable.

to do a Dutch—to run away

to get one's Dutch up—to arouse one's temper. Charles Earle Funke points out in his book *Heavens to Betsy* that this is, in fact, a reference to the Pennsylvania Dutch, who are of course not Dutch but German.

to be in Dutch—to be in trouble

The Dutch have done little to fight back. Noah Jacobs tells us in his books *Naming Day in Eden* that they do refer to a dirty trick in the Netherlands as a German trick and have been known to refer to the Scots in references to extreme cheapness. The only response, according to Stuart Berg Flexner, in *I Hear American Talking*, was in 1934 when the government of the Netherlands ordered its public officials to stop using the name *Dutch* because of its connotations and stick to *The Netherlands*.

If there is any consolation to the Dutch it is that they have been left out of the recent round of ethnic, geographical and college jokes (Newfie, Polack, Aggie, etc.) and that there are other ethnic slurs and characterizations. In 1944 Abraham Roback published a book entitled *A Dictionary of International Slurs*, which contained scads of them. Many of these ethnic and geographic terms are not slurs but descriptions used in everyday speech (French toast, Danish pastry, Chinese checkers, Siamese twins, Cuban heels, Canadian bacon, English muffins and so forth). Many of these are misnomers—Danish pastry is Vienna bread in Denmark and the English are unfamiliar with what Americans call English muffins—but they are hardly negative. On the other hand, we have:

American tweezers—burglary tools

Arizona tenor—cougher (who has gone to the Southwest for health reasons)

Chinese fire drill—pandemonium

German tea—beer

Indian gift—a gift that one expects to take back or to have returned

Italian perfume—garlic

Jewish penicillin—chicken soup

Mexican strawberries—beans

Norwegian Jello—*lutefisk*, so called because it is rubbery and gooey before cooking. It has been called far worse names.

Russian boots—leg irons

Scotch organ—cash register

Spanish padlock—chastity belt

Swedish fiddle—a cross-cut saw

Turkish medal—an unbuttoned fly

See also *Pennsylvania Dutch*.

E

Earth. *Earthling* seems to be the currently preferred demonym. It is, for example, the noun of "nationality" given in the CIA's *World Factbook* under the entry for "World." The CIA lists Earthlings as the appropriate adjective, but it is clearly not the one in use. The dominant adjective is Earth and shows up in constructions ranging from songs ("Earth Angel") to NASA satellites EROS (Earth Resource Observation Satellite). The term is capitalized when it refers to the name of the planet (the satellite went into Earth orbit), but not in applications like "down to earth." *Terrestrial* and *World* are common alternative adjectives.

It should be noted that not all *Earthlings* are thrilled with that name; for instance, those who are content to be called *human*. There are other possibilities. Futurist Ralph E. Hamil may have spoken for a number of people when he wrote the CIA to comment: "I think of myself as an Earthman. As a noun, Earthling has a diminutive tone; as an adjective, it is derogatory. I am more comfortable with it as a plural noun where the only alternative seems to be Earth People." Hamil has come up with a list of alternatives, including the standard English terms *Earthman/Earthwoman*, *Terrestrial* and *Earth People*, along with a number from science fiction, including the popular *Terran*, *Solarian* (a term that includes nearby worlds), *Terrestrial Being*, the facetious *Blue Planeteer* and the derogatory *Earthworm*. Sci-fi terms for the planet include *Terra* (used poetically like Dixie or Columbia), *Sol III*, *Blue Planet* and *Spaceship Earth*. Charles D. Poe has found a number of science-fiction names, including the compounds *Earth-person* and *Earth-human* and the rather nice sounding *Earther*.

East Asia. *East Asian*. The term *East Asia* is a synonym for *Far East* but less geocentric—the "far" in Far East is an allusion to its distance from Europe.

East Coast, USA. *Easterner*.

East Germany. *German*.

Ecuador (Republic of Ecuador). *Ecuadorean*. One finds examples of *Ecuadorean* and *Ecuadorian* in print. The nation takes its name from the Spanish *ecuador*, for "equator," which runs through the country, so the demonyms imply the idea of an equatorial person.

Edinburgh, Scotland, UK. *Edinburgher*.

Edmonton, Alberta, Canada. *Edmontonian*. Common personal nickname *Oiltowner*.

Egypt (Arab Republic of Egypt). *Egyptian. See* **United Arab Republic.**

Eire (Ireland). *Irish* or *Irishman/Irishwoman*.
  It has spawned some derivative words on the order of *Eirophiles* (people with a love for Ireland).

Elizabeth, New Jersey, USA. *Elizabethan*.

Ellice Islands. *Ellice Islander* (obsolete); now **Tuvalu**.

El Paso, Texas, USA. *El Pasoan*. H. L. Mencken noted that in names for citizens of American towns with Spanish names ending in -o that it was customary to drop the -o and add -an (*San Franciscan, Palo Altan, Sacramentan*, etc.), but that *El Pasoan* was the only exception he could find.

El Salvador (Republic of El Salvador). *Salvadoran,* although there is some use *Salvadorian.* The name of the Republic means "The Savior" in Spanish and its capital, San Salvador, means "Holy Savior."

Elsewhereian. Term created by former California Governor Goodwin Knight for residents of the state born outside it (elsewhere). It sounds like it would have become a generic term, but it does not appear to be used outside the Golden State.

Emirian. Resident of the United Arab Emirates.

England. *Englishman/Englishwoman.* Adjective: *English,* which appears in a number of constructions, from English sparrow to English muffin to English disease, an unflattering reference to chronic discontent and declining productivity. English also means a spin imparted to a ball to control its motion, such as the spin given to a billiard ball.

There has been some question as to when it is proper to use the term *England* and its derivatives when talking or writing about Britain or Great Britain. For instance, when *Forbes* magazine wrote about the Germans, Japanese, English and French in an editorial, a reader wrote to point out, "It is incorrect to call Britain 'England,' just as it would be to refer to Germany as Prussia, France as Burgundy, or Japan as Hokkaido" (December 15, 1986).

Perhaps, the best explanation comes in Henry Bradley and Robert Bridges' tract *Briton, British, Britisher,* "...the names *England* and *English,* the proper terms that differentiate the southern part of the island and its inhabitants from the northern Scotch and western Welsh parts and their inhabitants, have come to be used for the whole island and all the inhabitants thereof—thereby causing offence to those who wish to maintain their distinctive racial titles unobscured; *England* being thus like the name of the founder or predominant partner in a firm, which may hold onto his name even after his decease."

Épernay, France. *Sparnacien* (male), *Sparnacienne* (female).

Épinal, France. *Spinalien* (male), *Spinalienne* (female).

Equatorial Guinea (Republic of Equatorial Guinea, formerly Spanish Guinea). *Equatorial Guinean.*

Erie, Pennsylvania, USA. *Erieite.*

Eritrea, Ethiopia. *Eritrean.* An area as well as a separatist movement.

Estonia (Estonian Soviet Socialist Republic, constituent Republic of the Soviet Socialist Republics). *Estonian* or *Esthonian.* The shortened *Esth* is found in crossword puzzles (four-letter word for "Native of Tallinn"), but it seems to have little application outside that realm.

Ethiopia (Socialist Ethiopia). *Ethiopian.*

Eu, France. *Eudois.* In *"D'où Êtes-Vous* Revisited" (*Word Ways,* August 1986), the author is fascinated by this name because Eu began as Augusta, which has been whittled to a single vowel sound by linguistic attrition.

Eurasian. Person of European and Asian descent.

Europe. *European.* The question raised by this term is exactly which countries are "European." Are, for instance Great Britain and Iceland included? The answer varies depending on who is giving it.

Euro-. Prefix meaning European, which appears in seemingly countless constructions along the lines of Eurosclerosis (European economic slowdown), Europessimism (worries about Europe's economy) and Eurobashing (criticizing things European).

Evanston, Illinois, USA. *Evanstonian.*

Evansville, Indiana, USA. *Evansvillian.*

Exeter, England, UK. *Exonian*.

Exonian. Resident of Exeter, England. The term is also used for students and graduates of schools with Exeter in their name, for instances Phillips Exeter Academy.

Extraterrestrial. Being from outside the Earth's atmosphere; adjective for anything that is not of the Earth.

exurbanite. Generic term. Person living beyond the suburbs in the country who maintains urban ways. It gained popularity in the wake of a book, *The Exurbanites*, by A. C. Spectorsky (1955). His *exurbanites* were a displaced New York couple, disdainful of the suburbs, who moved farther out of town to live beyond their means. It spawned associated terms such as *ex-exurbanite* for one who returns to the city to live.

F

Falkland Islands (British colony of the Falkland Islands). *Falkland Islander*. This possession of the United Kingdom has been disputed territory since 1833. These islands are administered by the British but claimed by the Argentines, who call them the Islas Malvinas.

Far East. *Asian* is much more common than any derivative of Far East. *Far Eastern* is used as an adjective. East Asia is a synonym for Far East, preferred by those who see an element of Euro-centrism in the "far" (from Europe) of Far East.

This designation, along with Near East and Middle East, is not official, but generally applies to the easternmost portions of Asia. In order to bring order to vagueness, in 1952 the National Geographic Society specified it as "China, Mongolian Republic, Korea, Japan, the Philippines, Indochina, Thailand, Burma, Malaya and Indonesia."

Faeroe Islands/Faroe Islands. *Faeroese/Faroese.*

Far West, USA (Area west of the Rocky Mountains). *Westerner.*

fellow. Generic term. This word is demonymic in the sense of a construction like "fellow Americans," beloved of recent presidents who often address their audiences as "my fellow Americans." Occasionally, after this term is used by the president, the question is raised in newspaper letters and op-ed pages as to whether the adjective is one that excludes women because of the meaning of the word *fellow* for a man, boy or beau. One letter to the *Washington Post* after the term had been used by President Reagan suggested the alternative "My associate Americans" (August 26, 1987). If one is to base an answer to this question on the meanings given in standard dictionaries, it must be concluded that there are clear meanings of the term that are not linked to gender, in the sense of a fellow as peer, comrade or associate.

An interesting use of fellow is in the term *fellow traveler*, a phrase coined by Trotsky for a person who went along with communism without declaring himself as one—a closet communist. In his syndicated column "Words," Michael Gartner reveled in the irony of a form letter from a travel agency that began "Dear Fellow Traveler."

Fenwayite.   Baseball fan who frequents Boston's Fenway Park. It is an example of a special-case demonym.

Fernando Po.   *Fernandino*. However, Fernando Po is now called Bioko and it is part of Equatorial Guinea; hence *Equatorial Guinean*.

Fidéen.   Resident of Sainte-Foy, Quebec, Canada.

Fife (region), **Scotland, UK**.   *Man* or *Woman of Fife*. People from this area often refer to their realm as "The Kingdom of Fife."

Fiji.   *Fijian*. Sometimes *Fiji* is used as an adjective, as in Fiji rebels, but *Fijian* is more common.

Filipino.   Resident of the Philippines.

Finland (Republic of Finland).   *Finn. Webster's Ninth New Collegiate Dictionary* lists *Finlander* as its noun of choice, but it is, at best, a rarity—*Finn* is overwhelmingly favored. Adjective: *Finnish*. (Finnish is well suited to punning headline writers who use it as a play on finish, as in "Finish Line"—a *New Republic* article on a boycott by Finnair pilots [October 31, 1983].) Because of Finland's relationship with the Soviet Union, the term *Finlandization* has come to mean keeping a balance between independence and subservience.

Finn. Resident of Finland.

Flanders. *Flemish.*

Flint, Michigan, USA. *Flintite.*

Florence, Italy. *Florentine.* In culinary parlance, *Florentine* is applied to dishes served on a bed of spinach.

Florida (state), **USA.** *Floridian* is clearly proper while the rare *Floridan* is now without any broad support (even though the point is made from time to time that *Floridan* hews to convention and that *Floridian* is a resident of a place called "Floridia"). At one time, there were those who strongly favored *Floridan*, but by the time H.L. Mencken wrote his 1947 article "Names for Americans" the majority of the newspapers in the state had adopted *Floridian*.
COMMON PERSONAL NICKNAMES: Alligator, Cracker (*q.v.*), Everglader, Gator, Fly-Up-the-Creek and Gulfer.
COMMON NICKNAMES: Sunshine State, Gulf State, The Flowery State and St. Peter's Waiting Room (where part-time Floridian Ben Willis says, "...we senior denizens struggle to keep minds and bodies active while awaiting the Great Flight").

Formosa (The main island of Taiwan, which is also called Taiwan). The demonyms *Taiwanese* and *Chinese* are much more common than *Formosan*. This term has clear political overtones when referring to Formosa or *Formosans*. See **Taiwan.**

Fontainebleau, France. *Fontainbleen* or *Bellifontain.*

Fort Wayne, Indiana, USA. *Fort Waynite*.

Forth Worth, Texas, USA. *For Worthian*. However, the less popular and awkward-sounding *Fort Worther* has been cited in print and *Fort Worthan* has been spotted as close to the place in question as the *Houston Post* (June 27, 1988).

France (The French Republic). *Frenchman* or *Frenchwoman*. Adjective: *French*. In the English-speaking world the word *French* has been associated with sex; for instance, French kiss, French disease (syphilis) and French letter (a condom). However, many similar terms have no connection to the amorous arts, such as French fries, French doors, French cuffs, French horn, French toast, French beans etc.

Franco-Canadian. French Canadian (*q.v.*).

Franco-Ontarian. A Canadian of French ancestry living in Ontario, a province whose population is predominantly British in ancestry. The term has been given some prominence in discussions of constitutional rights denied to this minority: for instance, a headline in the February 7, 1982 *Manchester Guardian Weekly* reads "Raw deal for the Franco-Ontarians."

Frankfurt, Germany. *Frankfurter*.

French Canadian. Resident of Canada with French ancestry and/or whose native tongue is French.
    (It is spelled without a hyphen according to *The Associated Press Stylebook and Libel Manual*, making it an exception to the normal practice of hyphenating terms of dual ethnicity.)

French Guiana (Department of French Guiana). *French Guianese* or *French Guianan*. Adjective: *French Guiana*.

Frenchman/Frenchwoman. Resident of France.

French Polynesia (Territory of French Polynesia). *French Polynesian*.

French Territory of the Afars and Issas. See **Djibouti**.

French West Africa. *French West African*, now obsolete since French West Africa was divided into the independent states of Dahomey (now Benin), Ivory Coast, Mauritania, Niger, Guinea, Upper Volta (now Burkina Faso) and Mali.

Fresno, California, USA. *Fresnan*.

Friscan or *Friscoite*. Terms applied to residents of San Francisco, who probably view them with the same disdain they reserve for those who call the city Frisco. Writing under a San Francisco dateline, George Vecsey of the *New York Times* reported, "The locals call it The City and it's a $500 fine for any yokel who calls it Frisco."

Fujayrah (One of the United Arab Emirates). *Emirian*.

Futunan. Resident of the Wallis and Futuna Islands.

G

Gabon (Gabonese Republic). *Gabonese.*

Galena, Illinois, USA. *Galenian.*

Galesburg, Illinois, USA. *Galesburger.* (When Allen Walker Read, Professor Emeritus of English at Columbia University, was interviewed on the subject of Illinois names, he noted that you could buy a hamburger called a Galesburger in a restaurant there.)

Galicia (Province of Poland / Austria). *Galician.* Researcher Charles D. Poe has found the alternative *Galicianer* in print: "Undeniably, Galicianers were also clever, resourceful and determined..." (*Vengeance* by George Jonas, Bantam Books, 1984). Poe also found *Galitzianer*—pronounced *goll-itz-ee-on-er*—in Leo Rosten's *The Joys of Yiddish*, for a Jew from Galicia.

Galilee. *Galilean. Galilean* is also an adjectival derivative of the name Galileo.

Galloway, Scotland, UK. *Gallovidian*; however, *Galwegian* is often seen.

Galway, Ireland. *Galwayman/Galwaywoman*. Adjective: *Galway*, as in Galway Bay.

Gambia, The (Republic of The Gambia). *Gambian*.

Gary, Indiana, USA. *Garyite*.

Gas. Resident of Accra, Ghana.

Geneva, Switzerland. *Genevan* or *Genevese*.

Genoa, Italy. *Genoan* or *Genovese*.

Geordie. Resident of Newcastle upon Tyne, England; also *Tynesider*.

Georgia (state), **USA**. *Georgian*.
COMMON PERSONAL NICKNAMES: Buzzard, Cracker *(q.v.)*, Goober, Grabber and Sandhiller.
COMMON NICKNAMES. Peach State, Empire State of the South and The Cracker State.

Georgia (Georgian Soviet Socialist Republic, constituent Republic of the Union of Soviet Socialist Republics). *Georgian*.

Germany, East (German Democratic Republic). *German*, or *East German*. The use of *East German* is politically sensitive as East Germans do not refer to themselves this way. Adjective: *German*, as in German measles (rubella) or *Germanic*.

Germany, West (Federal Republic of Germany). *German* or *West German*. Adjective: *German* or *Germanic*. *Germanic* has a special connotation in that it is used to refer to that which is German in character.
  Germans from the Rhine area are sometimes called *Rhinelanders* and this term is sometimes incorrectly applied generally to any German. An interesting derivation is *Germania*, which was the name Adolf Hitler wanted to give Berlin after it had been modernized.

Ghana (Republic of Ghana, formerly Gold Coast). *Ghanaian.*

Gibraltar. *Gibraltarian.* Adjective: *Gibraltar.*

Gilbert Islands. *Gilbertese* (obsolete); now Kiribati.

Glasgow, Scotland, UK. *Glaswegian.*

Glendale, California, USA. *Glendalian.*

Goa. *Goanese.*

Godzone. Short for "God's Own Country," a chauvinistic name *New Zealanders* have bestowed on their country.

Gothamite.   Resident of New York City. In his *Phrase and Word Origins*, Alfred H. Holt points out that this term was first applied to New Yorkers in 1805 by Washington Irving. Holt explains,

> The inhabitants of Gotham, in England, had long been celebrated as fools (though one story has it that they got their reputation by playing the fool intentionally to avoid the expense of having to entertain the king). Irving's satirical application of the name to New York was an allusion to the Manhattanite's traditional air of "knowing it all." Gotham City is the home of comic book hero Batman.

Grand Rapids, Michigan, USA. *Grand Rapidian.*

Great Britain, or Britain (for short). (Consists of England, Scotland and Wales). *Briton.* See entries for **Britain, Briton, England** and **United Kingdom**.

Great Plains, USA (U.S. prairie lands that extend from the Missouri River to the Rocky Mountains and from North Dakota to Texas). *Plainsman/Plainswoman.*

Greece (Hellenic Republic/Republic of Greece). *Greek*. Adjective: *Greek, Hellenic* or *Grecian.*

Greensboro, North Carolina, USA. *Greensburgher.*

Greenland. *Greenlander*. Adjective: *Greenlandic.*

Grenada. *Grenadian.*

Guadeloupe (Department of Guadeloupe, French West Indies). *Guadeloupian* is the current choice, but *Guadeloupeen* can be found in earlier press accounts (e.g., *Christian Science Monitor*, May 7, 1949). Adjective: *Guadeloupe.*

Guam. *Guamanian*, not *Guaman.*

This demonym—with its double suffix—has an interesting history, which was outlined in a long letter that appeared in the September 1, 1950 issue of the *Washington Star* from Martha L. Jay of the *Guam Echo*. She wrote in response to a letter to the *Star* asking why Guamanians were called that. Her response in part:

> The native inhabitants of the Marianas Islands where Guam is located were originally known as Chamorros. However, after Guam came under the jurisdiction of the United States in 1898 and after the other Marianas Islands went to the Japanese under a League of Nations mandate at the end of World War I, the people of Guam assiduously cultivated Americans ways and philosophy. During World War II the Guamanians suffered hideously at the hands of the Japanese because of their loyalty to America and because of their many heroic deeds (not the least of which was the driving of the Japanese from one end of the Island of Guam).

> After World War II the people of Guam determined to separate themselves as distinctly as possible from those Chamarros who had been under Japanese jurisdiction between World War I and World War II. It was then that the Chamarros of Guam evolved the desire to be called Guamanians. There was, during the prewar period, some debate as to the relative merits of the names "Guamians," "Guamanians," and "Guamericans." Apparently, it was felt that "Guamanians" was more pleasing to the ear than either of the other two choices.

H

Hagenaar. Resident of The Hague, Netherlands.

Hague, Netherlands, The. *Hagenaar*.

Haiti (Republic of Haiti). *Haitian*.

Halifax, Nova Scotia, Canada. *Haligonian*. This North American demonym has a long history. Researcher David Shulman has found it in print as early as 1840 (*The United Service Magazine*, "…those days Haligonians were proverbial for their hospitality"). Shulman also found a 1859 example in which the term was spelled with two l's, but this must be considered an error or ephemeral variation.

Halluner Moat. Resident of Helgoland, the tiny North Sea island that during World War II was called "Hitler's Gibraltar." See **Helgoland**.

Hamburg, West Germany. *Hamburger*.

Hamilton, Ontario, Canada. *Hamiltonian* or *Hambletonian*. Traditional slang name is *Steeltowner*.

Hammond, Indiana, USA. *Hammondite*.

Beginning with the 1990 U.S. Census, *Guamanian* becomes one of the nine Asian-Pacific groups that a respondent can check off under the question of race (the others: Chinese, Filipino, Hawaiian, Korean, Vietnamese, Japanese, Asian-Indian and Samoan).

Guatemala (Republic of Guatemala). *Guatemalan* is the conventional choice, but *Guatemalteco* is used as well (as William Safire put it in his column of June 6, 1982, "When you're in Guatemala, do as the *Guatemaltecos* do").

Guianese. Resident of French Guiana.

Guinea (Republic of Guinea, formerly part of French West Africa). *Guinean*.

Guinea-Bissau (Formerly Portuguese Guinea). *Guinea-Bissauan*.

Guyana (Cooperative Republic of Guyana, formerly British Guiana). *Guyanese* (both singular and plural).

Hampshire (county), **England, UK**. *Hantsian*.

Hamptonite. Person who lives or vacations in one of the "Hamptons," several towns on eastern Long Island.

Hanover. *Hanoverian*.

Harrovian. Student or graduate of the famous Harrow school, Middlesex, Great Britain.

Hartford, Connecticut, USA. *Hartfordite*.

Hatter. Resident of Medicine Hat, Alberta, Canada.

Havana, Cuba. *Havanan*.

Hawaii (state), **USA**. *Hawaiian*, although *Islanders* is often used. For instance, the *World Almanac and Book of Facts* has a category for "Famous Islanders" under the entry for *Hawaii*. **Common Nickname**. Aloha State.

Hawkeye. Nickname for Iowa and, to a limited degree, an Iowan. For instance, the 19th-century editor and humorist Robert Jones Burdette was known as "The Burlington Hawkeye Man."

Hebrides, Scotland, UK. *Hebridean*.

Helgoland. *Helgolander*; however, one finds *Halluner Moat* as a name the islanders call themselves. Helgoland, in the North Sea, was evacuated by Hitler, who used it as a fort, and the islanders were not returned to their battered home until 1952. A 1952 Associated Press article on the return used both *Helgolander* and *Halluner Moat*. Helgoland is sometimes written as Heligoland with an i.

Hellenic. Adjective synonymous with Greek.

Helsinki, Finland. *Helsinkian*.

Herefordshire (former county), **England, UK**. *Herefordian*

Hermian. Term used by Arthur C. Clarke in his *Rendezvous with Rama* for a resident of the planet Mercury and as an adjective descriptive of the planet. This makes sense as Hermes was the Greek equivalent of the Roman god Mercury.

Herring Choker. Slang term for a resident of one of Canada's Maritime Provinces, especially a New Brunswicker. In *Columbo's Canadian References*, John Robert Columbo points out, "So plentiful are herring in the North Atlantic that the Atlantic Ocean was known in the late-seventeenth century as a 'herring pond.'" The term has also been used as a nickname for the Irish from County Galway.

Hertfordshire (county), **England, UK**. *Hertfordian*   (pronounced Hartfordian).

Hibbing, Minnesota, USA. *Hibbingite*.

Hibernian. Resident of Ireland. Adjective, which is synonymous with the word *Irish*.

Hispanic. Noun and adjective used to describe people of Spanish-speaking ancestry. In North America it is used as a catch-all for people with Spanish surnames whose families originally came from Spanish-speaking lands. The term is most useful because it is all inclusive. In an article in the February 1986 issue of *Word Ways*, the late Dmitri A. Borgmann compiled an admittedly incomplete list of 64 names (friendly, neutral and derogatory) for various *Hispanics* found in the United States, including *Afro-Cuban, Chicano* (and the female *Chicana*), *Cuban, Latin American, Mexican, Puerto Rican, South American, Spanish-Speaking* and *Spanish-Surnamed*.

Hispaniola (The island shared by Haiti and the Dominican Republic). *Hispaniolan*.

Hogtown. Traditional nickname for Toronto. *Hogtowner*.

Ho-Ho-Kus, New Jersey, USA. *Ho-Ho-Kusite*.

Hollywood, California, USA. Despite the importance of this Los Angeles suburb in the cultural scheme of things, there seems to be no common demonym. *Hollywoodite* is used, but rarely.

The name Hollywood inspires derivative words based on the idea of Hollywood as a source of glitz, glamour and fantasy. A *Hollywood ending* is a happy ending and to *Hollywoodize* is to give something added glamour. An interesting instance of the use of the verb came into play at the Democratic National Convention of 1960 when the finale (which included the acceptance speeches of John F. Kennedy and Lyndon B. Johnson) was said to be *Hollywoodized*.
COMMON NICKNAME: Tinseltown.

Holyoke, Massachusetts, USA. *Holyoker*, but sometimes the jocular *Holyokel* comes into play.

Honduras (Republic of Honduras). *Honduran*.

Hong Kong. *Hong Konger*.

Honolulu, Hawaii, USA. *Honolulan*.

Hoosier. Resident of Indiana. This term stands alone as an American demonym in terms of the concern and controversy it generates. It is a term that, if anything, is more popular today than ever before and is so universally preferred that it has totally eclipsed the old debate as to whether Indianian or Indianan was preferable.

The name appears everywhere. There are 107 businesses in the Indianapolis phone book whose names begin with Hoosier and that does not include the gigantic Hoosierdome. It is the nickname of the Indiana University basketball team and was the name of an immensely popular movie on Indiana high-school basketball. The Hoosier School of American Writing is one that included Booth Tarkington and James Whitcomb Riley, and to be called a *Hoosier's Hoosier* is to be paid the ultimate compliment.

"Hoosier English" is a term applied to the central-southern Indiana variety. In 1960 linguist Howard Whitchall, professor and one of the editors of *Webster's New World Dictionary*, predicted that it was just a matter of time ("perhaps 50 years") before it would be the dominant worldwide English accent. The speaker of Hoosier English says "feesh" for fish, "goood" for good and "greezee" for greasy.

Hoosier has more than one meaning. Before he became vice-president, Senator Dan Quayle made it very clear that he did not like those other non-Indiana meanings and actually took steps to take charge of the meanings of the term—to rewrite the dictionary definitions of *hoosier*.

The facts are these. On Monday, March 30, 1987, Senator Alfonse M. D'Amato of New York took the Senate floor and predicted that his alma mater, Syracuse University, would win the NCAA championship by beating the Indiana University Hoosiers that evening.

Such athletic boasts and jibes are common, and over the years the *Congressional Record* has detailed hundreds of them. However, in this case D'Amato invoked the sacred Indiana word of place, Hoosier, and pointed out that according to *Webster's Third New International Dictionary*, it not only meant a native of the state but also described "an awkward, unhandy or un-skilled person, especially an ignorant rustic." There was also a verb—*to hoosier*—which is defined as to "loaf on or botch a job." D'Amato used this verb to predict the defeat of Indiana: "I would submit to you that if that is the case...the outcome of the game tonight is a foregone conclusion and Syracuse will be victorious."

Neither of Indiana's senators was present for this, but Senator Robert Byrd of West Virginia did interrupt D'Amato to point out that Rule XIX of the Senate stated that a senator could be asked to take his seat if he spoke negatively of another state. Byrd asked D'Amato if he were speaking disparagingly of the state. "Of course not," D'Amato replied, "That would never be my intention."

That night Syracuse lost to Indiana by a score of 74-73.

The next day Indiana Senator Dan Quayle rose to the floor of the Senate to offer congratulations to the team and a nonbind-ing resolution containing a new definition of hoosier: "Whereas Indiana University's basketball team displayed the real mean-ing of the word, 'Hoosier,' therefore, be it resolved that a

Hoosier is someone who is smart, resourceful, skillful, a winner, unique and brilliant."

The matter could have rested at that point as a matter of spirited Senate tomfoolery in reaction to a championship season. However, Dan Quayle mentioned in his Senate speech that he intended to take up the definition he did not like with the editors of the dictionary. Later in the week, Quayle wrote to William A. Llewellyn, the president of the company that first published the mammoth *Merriam Webster's Third New International Dictionary* in 1961. The company, the Merriam-Webster Company of Springfield, Massachusetts, had published the first two editions in 1914 and 1934. Not without solid competition, this dictionary is regarded by many as the authoritative voice of American English. It is periodically updated through revisions and supplements.

Quayle asked that the old derogatory definitions be removed from the dictionary and suggested that his upbeat substitute be inserted. According to Llewellyn, Quayle also said that if the negative definitions could not be removed, at least a full explanatory discussion of the etymology of the term appear in the book.

Senator Quayle's office was given a polite but firm answer from Llewellyn in a letter that arrived on April 13. He added that the dictionary reflected the way words are used and that the company would be delighted to change the meaning if Quayle's meaning (quick, smart, resourceful, skillful, etc.) came into common use. Llewellyn later pointed out that his company's big dictionary is a "dictionary of record" and that it contains entries and definitions that people don't like. He added that the book contains four-letter words, racial and religious slurs and words that are regarded as sexist, for the simple reason that these words are part of the language. Also, it is not an etymological dictionary and there was no reason to afford *hoosier* special treatment.

In announcing Llewellyn's original reaction, Quayle's press secretary, Peter Lincoln, made a statement that was reported by the Associated Press: "We, and I'm sure the rest of the citizens of the Hoosier state, will press on with our campaign over time to persuade the folks at Webster's that they don't have it right." He also suggested a new verb, *to webster*, which he said meant "to misdefine a word stubbornly and out-rageously." An article by Lynn Ford of the *Indianapolis Star* appeared under the headline "Quayle may boot dictionary from his office" and reported that the book might be banned from Quayle's office. It quoted Lincoln as saying that a copy of the book was in the office, "But when the senator returns from vacation, I need to ask whether he wants a different dictionary in there." Reached a few days before Quayle was elected vice-president in 1988, Lincoln later said that the threat of banning the dictionary was done "tongue-in-cheek," but that the rest of the controversy was entirely "on the level." He said that he would stick by his definition of the verb, *to webster*.

Llewellyn said he did get about 50 letters on the subject of *hoosier*, of which about half sided with Quayle and the other half commended the dictionary for sticking to its definitions. Several came from people in such places as Kentucky and Missouri, who pointed out that *hoosier* was an insult in their neck of the woods and had nothing to do with the state of Indiana. Pamela N. Silva, the Merriam-Webster publicist, did check the company's file of more than 13 million citations on words and word usage and found that evidence dating back the 1850s showed the word hoosier was used in the U.S. South for "a lazy rustic."

Ironically, Quayle should have addressed his ire at the people of St. Louis and other places where the meaning of *hoosier* that obtains is closer to the meaning which offended the Indiana Republican. If anything, the dictionary treatment is mild com-pared to the reality in St. Louis. Listen to Elaine Viets, a popular columnist for the *St. Louis Post-Dispatch* who has written puck-ishly about Hoosier culture and once proposed a Hoosier museum replete with such artifacts as Confederate mud flaps and John Wayne portraits on velvet: "In St. Louis it has one meaning and that comes as a shock to people who come here from Indiana. It is highly pejorative and means a low life redneck." She points out that you don't call people hoosiers unless you want to get into a fight. "Hoosiers are destroyers: they get into fistfights and people are always calling the police about them. They have a car on concrete blocks in the front yard and are likely to have shot their wife who may also be their sister."

An article in the March 1987 issue of *Names: The Journal of the American Name Society* entitled "You $#"~*&@ Hoosier" by Thomas E. Murray of Ohio State University supports this definition and concludes that in the Gateway City it occupies "...the honored position of being the city's number one term of derogation."

The extensive file on the term in the Tamony Collection at the University of Missouri contains a number of negative applications of *Hoosier*, including use in sea slang (for an incompetent seaman), underworld slang (a sucker or hold-up victim), logger slang (fightin' word: stupid or cowardly), trade union jargon (anyone who doesn't know his job) and narcotics slang of the 1930s (a Hoosier fiend is an inexperienced addict who does not know of his addiction until deprived of drugs and then experiences withdrawal symptoms).

The word *hoosier* is of uncertain origin. A number of theories exist as to its origin, which makes it one of those curiosities that intrigue linguists. Several theories are consistent with the St. Louis version, including one that appeared in a handout from the Indiana Department of Tourism. The handout acknowledges an explanation offered by Hoosier poet James Whitcomb Riley, who said the term came from tavern fighting in which men would "gouge, scratch, and bite off noses and ears of their opponents. Then a settler would walk in and see an ear. He would ask, 'Whose ear?'" Another less than flattering theory is that it stems from the idea of a "husher"—a bully who hushes his opponents.

But these are a few of many. Some believe it to come from a Cumberland (England) dialect word, "hoozer," used for anything unusually large (the *humongous* of its time?) and others insist that it comes from a canal foreman named Hoosier who would only hire men from Indiana, and another says that it comes from the exclamation of victory "Huzza!"

In any event, the term has a long history. Its first literary appearance was in the *Indianapolis Journal* on January 1, 1833 in a poem by John Finley entitled "The Hoosier's Nest." It apparently sprang into use at once.

Houston, Texas, USA. *Houstonian.*

Hoya. Nickname for a student or graduate of Georgetown University, Washington, D.C. This term has caused much confusion because the standard dictionary definitions for *hoya* are: (1) a large genus of climbing Australian shrub and (2) a valley or basin high in the mountains. The university nickname stems from an earlier nickname for the football team, The Stone Walls. It seems that the team did not live up to that name and the students, with a touch of classic inspiration, renamed them the *Hoya Saxa*, which roughly translates to "What stones?" in a Latin-Greek mix. Later the name was shortened to *Hoya* or the *Hoyas*.

Hub. Nickname for Boston that is used as a noun (The Hub) and an adjective, as in "Hub union boss." Local newspapers use *Hub man* and *Hub woman* as alternatives to *Bostonian*.

Hungary (Hungarian People's Republic/Magyar People's Republic). *Hungarian*.

hyphenated American. Generic term. Name for Americans of family origin outside the United States. The term is used for this class of terms even when they are not actually hyphenated. For instance, in the discussion of *African American* following Jesse Jackson's 1988 call for its adoption, it was broadly referred to as "hyphenated."

I

Iberia (European peninsula containing Spain and Portugal). *Iberian*. Adjective is *Iberian*, although there are some exceptions such as Iberia Air Lines.

Ibiza, Spain. *Ibizan*.

Iceland (Republic of Iceland). *Icelander*. Adjective: *Icelandic*, as in Icelandic Airlines.

Idaho (state), **USA**. *Idahoan*, a term that long ago overwhelmed the little-used and academic *Idahovan*. H. L. Mencken wrote of it in his 1947 article "Names for Americans" in *American Speech*: "About 1925 the learned brethren of the State University at Moscow launched *Idahovan*, and for a while it was used in the university town press, but the rest of the State refused to accept it, and it has been obsolete since 1925."
COMMON NICKNAMES: Gem State and The Gem of the Mountains.

Illinois (state), **USA**. *Illinoisian*, but there is some support for *Illinoisan* or *Illinoian*. An article in New York's *Village Voice* on on the subject of demonyms (August 13, 1979) asserted that "anyone from Illinois is an Illinosan." The two-i *Illinosan* must be considered to be without any significant support.

The three choices here may underscore the point that all may be technically "correct," but that only one tends to be used. Confronted with the fact that the *Random House Dictionary*, second edition, unabridged (1987) lists all three, N. Sally Hass of Sleepy Hollow, Illinois, reacted, "Illinoisian (with the S pronounced) is the one we use around here. I've never heard the others. But the name of the state is *ill-annoy*, not *ill-a-noise*."

The term *Illini* us used for students and graduates of the University of Illinois. Hass, whose daughter attends the University, points out, "You'd think the singular would be Illinus (m.) or Illina (f.), but no. Illini is both singular and plural, masculine and feminine."

A University pamphlet entitled "The 80's Belong to the Illini!" reports, "The state of Illinois was named for an Indian tribe—Illini—which once inhabited the area. The term meant 'Brave Men.' Since the start of athletics at the state university in the late 1800's, the teams have ben called the 'Illini,' and more recently 'The Fighting Illini.'"

It seems that some Illinois residents are using *Illini* outside the context of the university. Philip Bateman of Decatur, Illinois, wrote to report that *Illinoisan* is generally regarded as proper, "But I hear Illini some among the general public—used either singular: 'I am an Illini' or plural: 'We are Illini.' Do not know if it will grow in use."

In an earlier time a resident of Illinois was a *Sucker* and it seemed to be mentioned in the same way that *Hoosier* is sometimes used for a person from Indiana. Other traditional nicknames for people from Illinois are *Sandhillers* and *Egyptians*, from the city named Cairo in the southern part of the state. *COMMON NICKNAMES*: Prairie State, The Inland Empire and The Sucker State.

Independence, Missouri, USA. *Independent*.

India (Republic of India/Sovereign Democratic Republic of India). *Indian*.

Indiana (state), **USA**. *Hoosier*. This term is discussed in detail under the entry for **Hoosier**. Despite the intensity of the Hoosier lobby the term *Indianan* still shows up in print, although it is usually followed by a letter to the publication in question asserting, as did a letter to the *Washington Post*, that "there is no such word as 'Indianan.'"
COMMON NICKNAME: Hoosier State.

Indianapolis, Indiana, USA. *Indianapolitan*.
COMMON NICKNAME: Ini.

Indianola, Mississippi, USA. *Indianolan*.

Indo-. Prefix for Indian used in such hyphenated terms as Indo-Aryan, Indo-Iranian and Indo-Hittite.

Indochina. *Indochinese*. This was the former French dependency that became Vietnam, Cambodia and Laos. The name is still used to refer to the three countries collectively.

Indonesia (Republic of Indonesia). *Indonesian*.

Iowa (state), **USA**. *Iowan*. Sometimes *Hawkeye* is used for an Iowan as well as for a student or graduate of the University of Iowa. This derives from the chief Black Hawk who figured in the early history of Iowa.
COMMON NICKNAME: The Hawkeye State.

Iran (Islamic Republic of Iran). *Iranian*. The nation used to be called Persia and the people Persians, but those terms are not used today. The language is *Farsi* but some outside the country still refer to it as Persian.

Iraq (Republic of Iraq). *Iraqi*. The modern nation coincides roughly with ancient Mesopotamia.

Ireland (Irish Republic/Eire). *Irishman/Irishwoman*. Collective plural is *Irish*. Adjective: *Irish*. An alternative demonym and adjective is *Hibernian* and the Irish are sometimes called *Patrick's People,* an allusion to St. Patrick.

In a derogatory sense Irish has been used in England and the United States for a certain crudeness, as in Irish confetti (bricks), Irish dividend (an assessment), Irish draperies (cobwebs), Irish parliament (a noisy argument bordering on a free fight) and Irish pennant (a loose thread). On the other hand there is Irish lace, Irish coffee and the Fighting Irish of Notre Dame University. Fighting Irish was originally the nickname of New York's heavily Irish 69th Regiment.

See also **Shanty Irish.**

Irish. Resident of Ireland (Irish Republic) and Northern Ireland, a part of the United Kingdom.

islander. Generic term for resident of an island.

In the case of Nantucket it would seem that *Islander* in the specific sense is used more often than *Nantucketer. Islander* appears with much more frequency in the island's newspaper the *Inquirer and Mirror.*

In some cases, anyone not from the island in question is known as an *Off-Islander.* Also the word is sometimes used in conjunction with a proper adjective, as in *Hawaiian Islander* or *Hebridian Islander.*

Islas Malvinas. See **Falkland Islands.**

Isle of Man, UK, The. *Manxman/Manxwoman.*

Israel (State of Israel). *Israeli.*

When the state of Israel was founded in early 1948, the National Geographic Society put out a press release that began:

> Washington, D.C.—The citizen of Israel should be called an Israeli, suggests the Foreign Secretary of the new Jewish state in Palestine. His preference follows an Arab-favored style which makes Iraqis of citizens of Iraq and Baghdadis of Baghdad's inhabitants.

The term was accepted immediately and without further debate, but the National Geographic Society could not resist pointing out that many other terms would have worked. It said that an Israeli could just as well have been "called an Israelian, in the manner of the Brazilian, Egyptian, or Babylonian. He could be an Israelese, following the form for the man from China, Japan, Siam, or Portugal. Taking a leaf from the book of the New Yorker, the Asiatic, the Frenchman, or the Nazarene, he could be respectively, an Israeler, an Israelic, Israelman or Israelene." It went on to say that even "Disraeli," the family name for the British prime minister, was a plausible alternatives, as was the time-honored Israelite.

The term *Israelite* has been relegated to biblical use and is an increasingly rare term for a Jew in an English-speaking nation. In the late 19th and the early 20th centuries there was a group of newspapers for American Jewish families named *The Israelites*, *The American Israelite* and *The Chicago Israelite*.

Istanbul, Turkey. *Istanbullu*.

Italy (The Italian Republic). *Italian*. The common adjective form is *Italian*, but *Italic* is used in talking about Italic language and italic typestyle.

Ivory Coast, The (Republic of the Ivory Coast, formerly part of French West Africa). *Ivorian*. There are some who use *Ivory Coaster*; however, sources ranging from the CIA's *World Factbook* to the *Washington Post* use *Ivorian*.

J

Jackson, Mississippi, USA. *Jacksonian.*

Jacksonville, Florida, USA. *Jacksonvillian.*

Jamaica. *Jamaican.* Adjective: *Jamaican,* but there is Jamaica rum.

Japan. *Japanese* (both singular and plural). Adjective: *Japanese,* but there is Japan Airlines.

The word *Japanese* should not be shortened to *Jap,* even as an abbreviation, as this is now universally regarded as a slur and nasty epithet. Books and movies of the World War II era contain this name, as it was a common wartime insult for a declared enemy. Despite the universal opposition to its use, the term still finds its way into print as an abbreviation.

In 1986 a concurrent resolution was passed by the House of Representatives in which the use of the abbreviation *Jap* was labeled as racially derogatory and offensive and it was suggested that Jpn (pronounced j-p-n) be used when an abbreviation is needed. The force behind such a resolution is moral rather than legally binding. Rep. Norman Y. Mineta (D-Cal.) made this point in supporting the resolution:

This abbreviation is so pervasive it still can be found in the word games of some major national newspapers, if not in their stylebooks. Newspaper usage is particularly important since most modern dictionaries list the offensive term at issue here as indeed an offensive racial epithet. Yet common usage has a powerful impact on society. And it is that usage we seek to influence with today's action.

Jarochos.   Resident of Veracruz, Mexico.

Jay Hawker/Jayhawker.   Common demonymic nickname for a Kansan. Kansas is the Jayhawk state and the Jayhawk is the mascot of the University of Kansas. In discussing this term in his *Good Words to You* the late John Ciardi described the modern mascot as: "A nonheraldic cartoon figure or stuffed doll of a nonexistent bird that resembles a miniature pterodactyl with a thyroid deficiency."

The original application of the term was anything but comic. It was used before the Civil War during the "Bloody Kansas" era as a nom de guerre for the free-soil guerrillas who fought the pro-slavery forces. Some of these original Jayhawkers were nothing more than criminals operating under the cover of chaos.

Because there is no such bird as the jayhawk, there have been many conjectural attempts to determine the inspiration for the mythical bird of prey. In his *Why Do Some Shoes Squeak?*, George W. Stimpson suggests a simple answer: it "may have been derived from a combination of the names of the blue jay and the sparrow hawk, both of which are plunderers."

Jefferson, Texas, USA.   *Jeffersonite.* C. F. Eckhardt points to the lack of parallelism here: "Folks from Houston have, since time out of mind, been called Houstonians, though those living in Jefferson have never been Jeffersonians but *Jeffersonites.*"

Jeffersontown, Kentucky, USA.   *Jeffersonian.*

Jersey (Channel Island), **England, UK.**   *Jerseyman/Jerseywoman/Jerseyite.*

Jersey City, New Jersey, USA.   *Jersey Cityite.*

Jerseyite/Jerseyman/Jerseywoman. Resident of the state of New Jersey. See **New Jersey**. Also resident of the Isle of Jersey (a British Channel island) whose people, in fact, founded and named what became the U.S. state.

Johannesburg, Republic of South Africa. *Johannesburger.*

Jordan (The Hashemite Kingdom of Jordan, formerly Transjordan). *Jordanian.*

Jovian. Adjective for the planet Jupiter. Used as a demonym in Emanuel Swedenborg's *The Earths in the Universe*. Writing about the psychic and medium who lived from 1688 to 1722, Martin Gardner described Swedenborg's Jovians as:

> kind and gentle, living on fertile lands where there are many wild horses. Although grouped into nations, warfare is unknown. Those in warm climates go naked except for loincloths. Their tents and low wooden houses have sides decorated with stars on blue backgrounds. When they eat they sit on the leaves of fig trees with their legs crossed. Curiously, they do not walk erect but 'creep along' by using their hands.

Swedenborg's description of other inhabitants of the sun's planets are no less curious and humanoid. *Mercurian* women, for instance, are small, beautiful and wear linen caps. All of these types are described in Gardner's article "Psychic Astronomy," which appeared in the Winter 1987 issue of *Free Inquiry*.

Jugoslav. Alternative term for resident of Yugoslavia. A short form is *Jug*, for a *Jugoslav* or *Jugoslavian*, which could easily be construed as derogatory even though it appears to be used in print as a short form on the order of *Brit* or *Balt*. "The Jugs denied everything," says a character in Paul Henissart's *Margin of Error*, "claimed it was a case of mistaken identity and personally put him on another plane..." One would be advised, however, to avoid its use if for nothing more than the simple reason that it has a jarring similarity to the defamatory *Jap*.

Jupiter (Planet). Adjective: *Jovian* (*q.v.*).

K

Kampuchea (Democratic Kampuchea). Short-lived name for Cambodia. *Kampuchean.* See **Cambodia**, as *Cambodian* was commonly used in the West when the name Kampuchea was in use.

Kansas (state), **USA**. *Kansan* is the formal demonym, but *Jay Hawker/Jayhawker* is the preferred nickname. See *Jay Hawker/Jayhawker* entry. Another traditional nickname for a Kansan is a *Sunflower*.
COMMON NICKNAMES: Jayhawk State, Sunflower State, The Central State (from its location on the map) and Prairie State.

Kansas City, Kansas and Missouri, USA. *Kansas Citian* or *Kansas Cityan*.

Kazakh Soviet Socialist Republic or Kazakhstan (Constituent Republic of the Union of Soviet Socialist Republics). *Kazakh.*

Kent, England, UK. A true oddity among demonyms because there are two forms depending on where one lives in Kent. As verified by reference librarian David S. Cousins of Canterbury, a *man of Kent* lives east of the River Medway while a *Kentish Man* lives west of the River Medway.

Kentucky (state), **USA**. *Kentuckian*. Charles D. Poe notes that this term has attracted its share of movie titles, including *The Fighting Kentuckian* (with John Wayne, 1949) and *The Kentuckian* (with Burt Lancaster, 1955). The derivative *Kentuckiana* for that which is typical or characteristic of Kentucky is in common use—for example, the annual Kentuckiana Antiques Market in Louisville.

Traditional slang names include, *Bear, Bluegrasser, Corn Cracker, Hardboot* and *Red Horse*.
COMMON NICKNAME: The Bluegrass State.

Kenya (Republic of Kenya). *Kenyan*.

Kerios. Resident of Athens, Greece, along with *Athenian*.

Kingston, Ontario, Canada. *Kingstonian*.

Kinshasa, Democratic Republic of the Congo. No common term in use; however, *Kinshasan* would seem logical.

Kirgiz or Kirghiz Soviet Socialist Republic (Constituent Republic of the Union of the Soviet Socialist Republics).*Kirgiz*.

Kiribati (Republic of Kiribati, formerly Gilbert Islands). *Kiribatian*. Adjective: *Kiribati*.

Kittsian. Resident of Saint Christopher and Nevis who can also be called a *Nevisian*. St. Kitts-Nevis is an alternative for the official St. Christopher and Nevis.

Kiwi. A *New Zealander*. The nickname parallels calling an *Australian* an *Aussie*. The kiwi is a flightless bird with hairlike plumage that is native to New Zealand. Kiwi fruit is also native to the nation. In the United States, the term is used with frequency in conjunction with New Zealand's participation in the America's Cup competition. "Kiwis' Challenge Is Accepted" read a headline in the *Sporting News* for December 14, 1987.

Knoxville, Tennessee, USA. *Knoxvillian.*

Korea, North (Democratic People's Republic of Korea). *North Korean.*

Korea, South (Republic of Korea). *South Korean.*

Kuril Islands (Area claimed by Japan but occupied by the Soviet Union since 1945). *Kurilian.*

Kuwait (State of Kuwait). *Kuwaiti,* according to the CIA's *World Factbook* and a number of contemporary newspaper citations, but *Kuwaytian* appears less frequently.

L

L.A. Common abbreviation/nickname for Los Angeles. It leads to some offbeat names such as *L-Aliens*.

Labrador, Canada (Region between Hudson Bay and the Atlantic Ocean). *Labradorean* or *Labradorian*. According to Alan Rayburn, writing in the *Canadian Geographic*, "*Labradorian* is a badge of honour for the longtime residents of Newfoundland living on the mainland side of the Strait of Belle Isle.

Ladakh, India. *Ladakhi*.

Lancashire (county), **England, UK**. *Lancastrian*. See **Lancaster** entry.

Lancaster, England, UK. *Lancastrian*. Roger B. Appleton of West Glamorgan points out that *Lancastrian* and *Yorkists* do not necessarily come from Lancaster or York. "The names originated in the 15th century when the two sides of the Royal Family fought what came to be known as the 'War of the Roses' to decide who really was who...Today a Lancastrian is a man from the whole county of Lancashire. A man from the county of Yorkshire is simply a Yorkshireman, sometimes shortened to the nickname 'Yorkie.'"

Lansing, Michigan, USA. *Lansingite.*

Laos (Lao People's Democratic Republic, formerly part of French Indochina). *Lao* or *Laotian.*

Lapland (An Arctic area extending through several nations). *Laplander*, for people residing in the area. The name *Lapp* is reserved for the nomadic people native to the area. Adjective: *Lapp.*

Laplander. 1. Resident of Lapland; a Lapp. 2. Person living on the Missouri-Arkansas border where Missouri "laps over" into Arkansas. In their book on Ozark folk speech, *Down in the Holler*, Vance Randolph and George P. Wilson note, "The 'bootheel' country in southeast Missouri has long been known as Lapland and is the subject of many dull jokes."

Las Vegas, Nevada, USA. *Las Vegan.* Resident Robert J. Throckmorton points out that the term *Vegasite*, which consciously apes the word "parasite," is used pejoratively and selectively.
COMMON NICKNAME: Vegas.

Latin America. *Latin American.*

Latino. A male Latin American; also an adjective for Latin American. *Latina* is the female form and used for Latin American women. As an adjective, Latino is used as a synonym for *Latin American.* Although the term *Hispanic* is often used as a synonym, such usage is not correct because Hispanic refers to all people of Spanish-speaking ancestry, including those from Spain.

Latvian Soviet Socialist Republic (Constituent Republic of the Union of Soviet Socialist Republics). *Latvian* or *Lett.* Adjective: *Latvian* or *Lettish.*

Lausanne, Switzerland. *Lausannois* (male), *Lausannoise* (female).

Lawrence, Kansas, USA. *Lawrentian*.

Lawrence, Massachusetts, USA. *Lawrencian*.

Lebanon (The Republic of Lebanon). *Lebanese*.

Leningrad, USSR. *Leningrader*.

Lesotho (formerly British Protectorate of Basutoland). *Mosotho* is the singular form while *Basotho* is plural. Adjective: *Basotho*. These terms are used in diplomacy; however, one can find *Lesothan* in novels and newspapers. The vernacular language of 99 percent of the people is *Sesotho*.

Lett. Resident of Latvia

Lettish. Adjective for Latvia; *Latvian*.

Lexoviens. Resident of Lisieux, France.

Liberia (Republic of Liberia). *Liberian*.

Libya (Socialist People's Libyan Arab Jamahiriya). *Libyan*.

Liechtenstein (Principality of Liechtenstein). *Liechtensteiner*. Adjective: *Liechtenstein*.

Lilliputian. Adjective for a diminutive person or object which comes from the fictional Lilliput of Jonathan Swift's *Gulliver's Travels*.

Lima, Peru. *Limeños*.

Limey/Limejuicer. Increasingly archaic American term for Briton. It seems to have begun with American sailors noting the compulsory British practice of giving sailors lime juice as an antiscorbutic, although there is some evidence to support the idea that it derives from the expletive "God blim'y" (for God blame me). From an American standpoint, the term seems to have begun as a seagoing slur but later was more commonly used with some degree of affection, such as during the two world wars.

Limoges, France. In *"D'où Êtes-Vous* Revisited" (*Word Ways*, August 1986) we are told, "An inhabitant name which in the feminine form has become an English noun is Limousine (from Limoges, which also has limougeaud.)"

Lincoln, Nebraska, USA. *Lincolnite.*

Lincolnshire (county), **England, UK.** *Lindurian* in some circles, according to the research of Jay Ames, but *Lincolnian* in others.

Lisbon, Portugal. *Lisboan.*

Lisieux, France. *Lexoviens.*

Little Rock, Arkansas, USA. The prevailing name for a resident of Little Rock is *Little Rockian.*

Lithuania (Lithuanian Soviet Socialist Republic, constituent Republic of the Union of Soviet Socialist Republics). *Lithuanian.*

Liverpool, England, UK. *Liverpudlian*, which is conventional, but also the slang nickname *Scouse* or *Scouser.*

Liverpudlian is apparently based on 17th-century punning. The *Oxford English Dictionary* says the term dates from 1833 "from Liverpool (with joc. substitution *puddle* for *pool*) + IAN." One finds some cases in which it is spelled *Liverpuddlian*, such as Robert W. Chapman's *Adjectives from Proper Names.*

Phillip Chaplin, who has done research on *Scouse* and *Scouser*, reports, "Lobscouse is the name of a dish of salt beef biscuit and onions formerly common in British merchant ships. I believe the American equivalent was cracker hash. Shortened it means a native of Liverpool, which is, of course, a major commercial port."

London, England, UK. *Londoner.*

Long Beach, California, USA. *Long Beacher.*

Longwy, France. *Longovicien* (male), *Longovicienne* (female).

Looper. Resident who works in Chicago's Loop, an example of how these geographical nouns can work down to the neighborhood level.

Los Angeles, California, USA. *Angeleno* and *Angelino* are the most commonly used terms, but one also finds *Los Angeleno* and *Los Angelean.* Derivatives are rare, but one finds examples of *Losangelize* for creating something in the image or style of the city. Motion picture director Mike Nichols described his 1967 film *The Graduate* as being about "the Losangelization of the world" (the *San Francisco Examiner*, July 24, 1967). There was also a bumper sticker selling in Marin County, California, in the mid-1970s that read DON'T LOSANGELIZE MARIN (this, in turn, prompted a counter-sticker, DON'T MARINATE LOS ANGELES).

Los Angeles has attracted a number of nicknames ranging from the neutral *L.A.* to the deprecating *Lotusland*, *Lotusville* and *Lalaland*. The *Lotus-* names and *Lalaland* are often used in the context of a grotesque event. The *San Francisco Chronicle* used to run such items as stories about fistfights between Hollywood stars under the headline "Life in Lotusland Department." One of the oddest nicknames for the city was *Double Dubuque*, a put-down popular in the years following World War II through the 1960s.

Louisiana (state), **USA.** *Louisianian* or *Louisianan.* Most press and book citations favor *Louisianian*, but one can find *Louisianan* in the pages of the *New York Times* ("Louisianans Rally to Win I- AA Title," a sports section headline, December 21, 1987). One historic nickname is *Pelican*. See also entry for **Cajun**.

COMMON NICKNAMES: The Pelican State and The Creole State.

Louisville, Kentucky, USA. *Louisvillian*.

Low Countries (Collective name for Belgium, Luxembourg and the Netherlands). No commonly accepted demonym.

Lubbock, Texas, USA. *Lubbockite*.

Lunar. Of the Moon (*q.v.*).

Lusitania (Ancient name for what is now central Portugal). *Lusitanian*. The term is sometimes used as a noun or adjective synonym for *Portuguese*.

Luxembourg/Luxemburg (Grand Duchy of Luxembourg). *Luxembourger*, which seems to be the preferred form, or *Luxemburger*. The French version is *Luxembourgeois*, which appears in the *Oxford English Dictionary*. This tiny nation has the distinction of a relatively large group of acceptable adjectives—*Luxembourg, Luxembourgeois, Luxembourgian* and *Luxemburgian*.

Lyons, France. *Lyonnais* (male), *Lyonnaise* (female). *Lyonnaise* is used in a culinary context for food prepared with sautéed onions.

M

Macao or Macau. *Macanese* (both singular and plural). Adjective: *Macau*. Chinese territory, west of Hong Kong, under Portuguese administration.

Madagascar (Democratic Republic of Madagascar). *Malagasy* (both singular and plural). *Webster's Ninth New Collegiate Dictionary* gives *Madagascan* as both the noun and adjective while the CIA's *World Factbook* gives only *Malagasy*. (*Madagascan* may be technically correct but the "gas can" ending sounds odd.)

Madison, Wisconsin, USA. *Madisonian*.

Madras, India. *Madrasi*.

Madrid, Spain. *Madrilenian* or *Madrileño*.

Maggie. Female *Aggie* (*q.v.*).

Maine (state), **USA**. *Mainer* or *State of Mainer*. Another term, *Maineiac*, or its alternative *Mainiac* or *Maine-iac*, is used affectionately for summer residents who fall in love with the place or immigrants who stick around. An anecdote in the December 1983 *Reader's Digest* from a Hampden, Maine, man told of a native explaining the difference between *Mainer* and *Maine-iac*:

"A 'Mainah' is a pehson who likes Maine so much that he decides to stay through the wintah. A 'Maine-iac' is a person who is so devoutly in love with Maine that he decides to stay a second wintah." In his incomparable *Maine Lingo*, John Gould notes that "*Maineiac* is more used by out-of-staters than by bona fide residents of the Pine Tree Precinct, but the latter are capable of tossing it off to describe themselves when it suits, and with more than a little pride." A parody newspaper produced in Maine beginning in 1987 is called the *Maineiac Express*.

Historic nicknames and slang terms include *Fox*, *Logger*, *Lumberman* and *Pine Treeman*.

See also **Down East**.

COMMON NICKNAMES: Pine Tree State, Down East State and The Lumber State.

Majorca, Spain. *Majorcan*.

Malaga Islandite. A demonym with a special meaning in Maine, where it once was euphemistic for a misfit. It shows up in John Gould's *Maine Lingo* with the following explanation:

> About the turn of the century unpleasant conditions among the residents of Malaga Island in eastern Casco Bay forced the state welfare authorities to resettle them by families in numerous Maine communities. It was a social-betterment project well ahead of its time. Historically, Malaga Island has been a dumping place for odd people brought to Maine from the waterfronts of the world, with consequent confusion.

Malagasy. Resident of Madagascar (Democratic Republic of Madagascar).

Malagasy Republic. See **Madagascar**.

Malawi (Republic of Malawi). *Malawian*.

Maldive Islands/Maldives (Republic of Maldives). *Maldivian*.

Mali (Republic of Mali, formerly French colony of Sudan). *Malian* or *Mali*.

Malouin/Malouine. Resident of Saint-Malo, France.

Malta (Republic of Malta). *Maltese* (both singular and plural).

Manchester, England, UK. *Mancunian.*
The term has been said to derive from Mancunium, the name of a Romano-British town on the site, but the *Encyclopedia Britannica* says there was no town (though there was a fort nearby, name uncertain, perhaps Mancunium or Mamucium).

Manhattan Island, New York, USA. *Manhattanite.* See also *Gothamite.* The derivative *Manhattanitization* describes the process of becoming like the island between the Hudson and East rivers. The specific meaning varies with the context, but it is often used to describe the growing number of high-rise buildings. It has also been used to mean urban decay.

Manila, Philippines. *Manilite.*

Manitoba (province), **Canada.** *Manitoban.*

Manitou Springs, Colorado, USA. This matter prompted what was one of the most interesting letters attracted by the demonym project. It came from Susan Elizabeth Musick of Norman, Oklahoma and it reads:

> As one who has moved around the country a bit, I've had a fair number of what Paul Dickson calls "demonyms." I was born an Illinoisan—a Lockporter to be exact—and it was early impressed on me that the S in Illinoisan is silent. I've been a San Franciscan—which is by no means your run-of-the mill Californian, and almost a different specials from an Angeleno. I've been an Oregonian, but was told by some there that I ought to call myself a Webfoot. For nineteen years I was a Coloradan, putting in time as a Denverite, a Colorado Springsite, and a Cripple Creeker in addition to the time I spent in Manitou Springs. Then last year I became an Oklahoman, or, as many insist, a Sooner. But my favorite of all demonyms is what my neighbors in Manitou Springs called themselves: *Manitoids.*

Manx. Adjective for the Isle of Man and the name of breed of cat that has a bump where its tail should be. The cat originated on the island and many are still bred there at the government-owned Manx Cattery in the Manx capital of Douglas.

Manxman/Manxwoman.   Resident of the Isle of Man.

Mariel, Cuba. *Marielito*. Name given to the 125,000 Cubans who were sent from Mariel, a city on Cuba's west coast, to the United States in 1980 as "outcasts." The vast majority of the *Marielitos* have been assimilated into American society, but the term still exists to identify those who were in the mass boat lift.

Marin County, California, USA. *Marinite*.

Maritime Provinces, Canada (Nova Scotia, New Brunswick and Prince Edward Island collectively). *Maritimer*; also the slang term *Herring Choker*.

Marseilles, France. *Marseillais* (male), *Marsellaise* (female).

Marshall Islands (Pacific Trust Territory). *Marshallese*.

Marshall, Texas, USA. *Marshallite*.

Martha's Vineyard, Massachusetts, USA. *Vineyarder*.

Martinique (French Overseas Department of Martinique). *Martiniquais* (both singular and plural), according to the CIA's *World Factbook*, but the book *Liverpudlian* says *Martican*.

Maryland (state), **USA**. *Marylander*. Coming off the tongue of a native, this demonym, which has shown up in print as early as 1723, sounds more like "Merl-lander" than "Mary-lander." The derivative for that which is typical or characteristic of the state is *Marylandia*. Historic nicknames and slang terms include *Cockader, Crawthumper, Old Liner, Oyster* and *Terrapin*.
COMMON NICKNAMES: Free State or Old Line State. The latter name comes from colonial days when Maryland refused to alter its boundaries to please Lord Baltimore and William Penn.

Massachusetts (nominally a state, but legally a commonwealth), **USA**. *Bay Stater*. An early scholar who looked at the process of naming citizens in 1859 threw up his hands and announced that Massachusetts, Connecticut and Arkansas refused to yield to the process. Attempts have been made to give names on the order of *Massachusettite* and *Massachusettsan* but they have not taken. Newspapers in the commonwealth occasionally yield examples deriving directly form its name, but they seem to be created for effect or alliteration, as in the "meddlesome *Massachusettsensian*" spotted in the *Boston Herald* and the "inevitable *Massachusettsian*," an allusion to Senator Ted Kennedy in the *National Review*. Despite all of this, the official name used by the Government Printing Office is *Massachusettan*.

Historic nicknames and slang terms include *Baked Bean*, *Old Colonial* and *Puritan*.
COMMON NICKNAMES: Bay State, Old Bay Colony, Old Colony and "Taxachusetts" (for its higher-than-average tax rates).

Mauritania (Islamic Republic of Mauritania, formerly part of French West Africa). *Mauritanian*.

Mauritius. *Mauriitian*.

Melbourne, Australia. *Melburnian*.

Medicine Hat, Alberta, Canada. *Hatter*, but also Medicine Hatter.

Memphis, Tennessee, USA. *Memphian* or *Memphite*.

Man/Woman of Fife. Resident of Fife, Scotland.

Mercury (Planet). *Mercurian*. Adjective: *Mercurial*.

Mesopotamia (Ancient kingdom that is now part of modern Iraq). *Mesopotamian*.

Messin. Resident of Metz, France.

Metz, France. *Messin.*

Mexico (United States of Mexico). *Mexican.*

Mexico City, Mexico. *Chilango* or *Mexicano.*

Miami, Florida, USA. Miamian.

Michiana, USA (Unofficial name for the area surrounding South Bend, Indiana, where northern Indiana and southern Michigan meet). *Michianan.*

Michigan (state), **USA.** *Michiganian* is the official name, but some strong support exists for *Michigander.*

In 1979 the state legislature voted to make *Michiganian* the official name. The bill was introduced at the urging of newspaper editors who were confused by a variety of names, including "Michigander," "Michiganite" and "Michiganer." Some citizens will continue to call themselves Michiganders, a term that legend has it, was created by Abraham Lincoln in the 1848 presidential campaign. It is also the name given by H. L. Mencken in *The American Language.* However, because of the *-gander* in the term, it suffers some from those who puckishly insist, "If the men are *Michiganders*, the women are *Michigeese*."

Michiganite is given in the GPO *Style Manual* and was put there by the GPO Style Board. This term has been fought by residents for years. An article in the *Christian Science Monitor* from December 19, 1957 points out that there were many in the state who wished the government in Washington would leave the name alone. An executive of the Michigan Tourist Council was quoted as saying that *Michiganite* "sounds like something you'd dig out of the ground." That executive, Robert Furlong, favored *Michiganian* because it "just plain sounds better. It has a roll and a savor to it." (*Webster's Ninth New Collegiate Dictionary* lists *Michiganite* as an alternative to *Michigander.*)

All of this debate over the proper name for a person from Michigan suggests a certain zaniness that was underscored in a letter from Brooklynite Lillian Tudiver, "I am sure that this is

one of many letters you have received pointing out that Michiganer or Michiganah [sounds like a word that] means a crazy person in Yiddish." The nickname of the state and its residents is *Wolverine*, which appears to have been used more commonly in the past. Historic nicknames and slang terms include *Wolverine* (*q.v.*).
COMMON NICKNAMES: Wolverine State, The Lake State and The Automobile State.

Middle Atlantic States, USA. (The U.S. Census Bureau defines these as New York, New Jersey and Pennsylvania, but some less formal references include Delaware.) *Middle Atlantian.*

Middle East/Mideast (Collective name for a group of nations: Afghanistan, Iran, Iraq, Israel, Kuwait, Jordan, Lebanon, Oman, Qatar, Saudi Arabia, South Yemen, Syria, Turkey, United Arab Emirates, Yemen, Egypt, Sudan and Cyprus). *Middle Easterner* or *Mideasterner*. The term now includes the area once considered to be the Near East, which is now hard to distinguish from the term *Middle East*. In 1952, the National Geographic Society, trying to bring order to the three Easts (Near, Middle and Far), limited its definition of the Middle East to India, Pakistan, Afghanistan, Nepal, Bhutan, Sikkim and Ceylon.

Middle West/Midwest, USA (Collective name for the states of Indiana, Illinois, Michigan, Ohio, Wisconsin, Iowa, Kansas, Minnesota, Missouri, Nebraska, North Dakota and South Dakota). *Midwesterner* or *Middle Westerner*. Adjective: *Middle Western* or *Midwestern*.

Milan, Italy. *Milanese*.

Milwaukee, Wisconsin, USA. *Milwaukeean*.

Minneapolis, Minnesota, USA. *Minneapolitan*.

Minnesota (state), **USA**. *Minnesotan*. A historic nickname is *Gopher*.
COMMON NICKNAMES: North Star State and Gopher State.

Mississippi (state), **USA**. *Mississippian*. Historic nicknames and slang terms include *Bayou, Border Eagle, Mud Cat, Mud Waddler* and *Tadpole State*.
COMMON NICKNAMES: The Bayou State and The Magnolia State.

Missouri (state), **USA**. *Missourian*. Historic nicknames and slang terms include *Doubting Thomas* (presumably from the "Show Me" motto), and a nickname for a resident of this state that was extremely common in the 19th century, *Puke* (*q.v.*). Still another archaic and pejorative name for Missourian is *Piker*. It has been suggested that it came from the days of the California Gold Rush because so many Missourians came from Pike County, but it may also be related to *Puke(r)*.
   Because Missouri is the "Show Me State" the term *Missourian* has been used for anyone who has to be shown proof. An ad in the Tamony Collection for a betting system beings with the line: "ALL MISSOURIANS—DOUBTERS—SKEPTICS—LOS-ERS!!" (*The National Police Gazette*, September 27, 1924).
COMMON NICKNAME: Show Me State.

Mobile, Alabama, USA. *Mobilian*.

Moldavian Soviet Socialist Republic (Resident Republic of the Union of Soviet Socialist Republics). *Moldavian*.

Monaco (Principality of Monaco). *Monegasque* (pronounced MONEY-gasque) or *Monacan*.

Monegasque.   Resident of Monaco (MONEY-gasque).

Mongolia (Mongolian People's Republic). *Mongol*. The CIA's *World Factbook* says *Mongolian*.

Montana (state), **USA**. *Montanan*. One nickname that has been used is *Stubtoe*.
COMMON NICKNAMES: Mountain State and Treasure State.

Montenegro (Federated Republic of Yugoslavia). *Montenegrin*.

Montevideo, Uruguay. *Montevideans*.

Montreal, Quebec, Canada. *Montrealer,* but Montréalais/-Montréalaise in French.

Moon. *Lunarian* has been suggested for a resident but *Selenite* seem to have strong support. Futurist Ralph E. Hamil, who prefers the latter, points out that *Selenite* is basically the same in French, Spanish and Russian. This is not as academic as it may seem because while the population may be zero, it has been as high as two. *Lunar* is the preferred adjective.

Moonraker. Resident of Wiltshire, UK. It is one of those British demonyms with a charming story behind it. The nickname derives from a tale of the area in which local lads were smuggling in some untaxed brandy late one moonlit night when an excise man surprised them. To avoid detection, they were forced to roll the barrels of brandy into a pond. They dumped the brandy in time and the tax man left, but the excise man returned later and caught the lads using huge hay rakes to retrieve their contraband. The smugglers explained that they were dragging the pond for a large cheese they had spotted and pointed to the reflection of the full moon on the surface of the pond. The revenuer left convinced that these men—these "moonrakers"— were daft.

Moose Jaw, Saskatchewan, Canada. *Moose Javian.* Geographer Alan Rayburn notes that this does not conform to any established pattern "...although it may be related to Shavian, the literature of George Bernard Shaw."

Morocco (Kingdom of Morocco/Kingdom of the West). *Moroccan.*

Moscow, Idaho, USA. *Moscowite.*

Moscow, USSR. *Muscovite.*

Mosotho. See **Lesotho.**

Motown. Nickname for Detroit, Michigan, which is also used adjectivally: *Motown sound.* Also, Motor City.

Motswana. Resident of Botswana (Republic of Botswana) in the singular, but *Botswana* is the plural form, according to the CIA's *World Factbook*. *Botswani* is also used.

Mozambique (People's Republic of Mozambique).   *Mozambican.*

Muncie, Indiana, USA. *Muncieite.* An interesting note on this came from Baltimorean Melvin H. Wunsch:

> When I lived in Muncie, Ind., 45 years ago, I wrote to [H. L.] Mencken about *The American Language*. When he replied, he asked what residents of Muncie called themselves.
>
> I checked and told him that "Muncieite" seemed to be preferred over "Muncian" and that, years earlier, "Munsonian" had been suggested. I added that the place had been named after the Munsee tribe of Indians. He expressed surprise at that in his thank you note and added that he had always assumed the city had been named after Frank Munsey, the world's worst editor.

Muscat and Oman (Sultanate of Muscat and Oman).   *Muscati* and *Omani.*

Muscovite. Resident of Moscow, USSR.

Myanma (Pronounced Mee-ahn-ma). *Myanman.* The nation was known as Burma until 1989. The ethnic majority in the country are still Burmese and individuals may be identified as such.

N

Nairobi, Kenya. *Nairobian*.

Namibia (Formerly South West Africa). *Namibian*.

Nantucket, Massachusetts, USA. *Nantucketer* seems to be more popular off the island than on it (*New York Times* headline of May 24, 1987 reads, "Nantucketers Adapting to Development Woes"). *Islander* seems to be preferred on Nantucket and in the local newspaper, the *Inquirer and Mirror*. See also entry for *off-islander*.

Nassau, Bahama Islands. *Nasauuian* or *Nassauian*.

Naples, Italy. *Napoletano*. Adjective: *Neapolitan*.

national. Generic term. Person living away from the nation in which he or she is a citizen, or a person under the protection of another nation. For instance an American in the Soviet Union would be regarded as an "American national."

native. Generic term. Person born in a given location, such as an indigenous New Yorker. The term carries a sense of permanence that does not come with *resident* or other terms of location.

Nauru (Republic of Nauru). *Nauruan.*

Nashville, Tennessee, USA. *Nashvillian* or *Nashvilleite.*

Naxalbar, West Bengal, India. *Naxalite.*

Nazareth, Israel. *Nazarene.* Jesus Christ is sometimes referred to as "The Nazarene."

Neapolitan. Resident of or adjective relating to Naples, Italy.

Near East. *Near Easterner.* The term *Near East* has suffered an identity crisis as it is hard to distinguish from the term *Middle East*. As defined by the National Geographic Society, which tried to bring order to the three Easts (Near, Middle and Far) in 1952, the area includes Turkey, Cyprus, Syria, Lebanon, Israel, Iraq, Iran, Egypt, Jordan and the Arab Peninsula nations.

Nebraska (state), **USA**. *Nebraskan*, although the nickname *Cornhusker* is common. Other traditional nicknames include *Antelope* and *Bug Eater*.
COMMON NICKNAMES: Cornhusker State and Beef State.

Neorican. Puerto Rican who lives in the continental United States or has lived on the mainland and returned to the island.

Nepal (Kingdom of Nepal). *Nepalese* (both singular and plural).

Netherlands, The (Kingdom of the Netherlands). *Dutch* is informal. *Netherlander* is listed by the CIA's *World Factbook* and *Webster's Ninth New Collegiate Dictionary*. Adjectives: *Netherlands* and *Dutch*. The news media tends to use *Dutch*, as in a Dutch tanker or the Dutch army. See entry for **Dutch**.

Netherlands Antilles. *Netherlands Antillean.*

Nevada (state), **USA**.   *Nevadan.* The term *Silver Stater* is used but is far less common than *Nevadan*. Historic nicknames and slang terms include *Digger*, *Miner*, *Sagebrusher* and *Sage Hen*. *COMMON NICKNAMES*: Silver State and Sagebrush State.

Nevisian.   Resident of Saint Christopher and Nevis, which is also known as St. Kitts-Nevis.

Newark, New Jersey, USA.   *Newarker.*

New Brunswick (province), **Canada**.   *New Brunswickian* and *New Brunswicker* are common, but *Herring Choker* is a common nickname that apparently is not as derogatory as it sounds.

New Caledonia (Territory of New Caledonia and Dependencies).   *New Caledonian.* Because Caledonia is the Latin name for Scotland, it would be incorrect to call a resident of New Caledonia a *Caledonian*, a name reserved for Scots.

Newcastle, New South Wales, Australia.   *Novocastrian.*

Newcastle-upon-Tyne, England, UK.   Several terms are used: the formal *Novocastrian*, the much more popular *Tynesider* (from the name of the city's river) and *Geordie*. The latter name is an affectionate form of George. The reason that it was first applied to people of this area has been obscured by time.

New Delhi, India.   *Delhite.*

New England, USA.   *New Englander* and the nickname *Yankee* (*q.v.*). *New Englandy* and *Yankee* are adjectives.

Newfoundland (province), **Canada**.   *Newfoundlander.* The alternative *Newlander* was advanced by newspaper writers after World War II, according to an Associated Press dispatch of October 13, 1948, because the residents objected to the slang terms *Newf* and *Newfie*. Despite this, the slangy *Newfie* is still in common use, such as in informal travel articles.

New Hampshire (state), **USA**. *New Hampshirite*; however, *New Hampshireman/New Hampshirewoman* or, simply, *Hampshireman/Hampshirewoman* are traditional and listed as the terms of preference in some dictionaries. *Granite Boy/Girl* is an old slang term for a native.
COMMON NICKNAME: Granite State.

New Haven, Connecticut, USA. *New Havener.*

New Hebrides. See **Vanuatu**.

New Jersey (state), **USA**. *New Jerseyite*, although *New Jerseyan* does show up frequently in print. For instance, a letter published in the *National Review* (June 10, 1988) from a New Jersey man talks of a piece of legislation that "allows New Jerseyans to deduct part of their property tax from their state income tax." *Jerseyan* and *Jerseyite* are sometimes used when there is no chance of confusion with the British Isle of Jersey. Earlier writers often used *Jerseyman* and *Jerseywoman*, which are rare today, but used proudly by some traditional natives.

Historic nicknames and slang terms include *Blue, Clam, Clam Catcher* and *Jersey Blue State.*
COMMON NICKNAME. The Garden State.

New Mexico (state), **USA**. *New Mexican.*

An interesting derivative is the style of cooking known as *New Mex,* for a combination of New Mexican and Mexican influences in the manner that *Tex Mex* cooking combines Texan and Mexican.
COMMON NICKNAME: Land of Enchantment.

New Orleans, Louisiana, USA. *New Orleanian* or *Orleanian,* although some use *Orleenian.*
COMMON NICKNAME: The Big Easy.

Newport, Kentucky and Rhode Island, USA. *Newporter.*

Newport News, Virginia, USA. There is no commonly accepted term in use.

New South Wales (state), **Australia**. *New South Welshman* as well as *Cornstalk*, according to Australian folklorist Bill Scott. The latter should be used with caution, as pointed out in the entry for *Banana-Bender* (*q.v.*).

New Town/new town. Any of a number of planned communities with controlled growth, such as Reston, Virginia, Columbia, Maryland, and Tapiola, Finland. *New Towner*.

New World (North and South America and surrounding islands). *New Worlder*.

New York (state), **USA**. *New Yorker*.
   It is occasionally suggested that New Yorkers deserve a more colorful name (on the order of *Hoosier* or *Sooner*), but none has ever come along. In this regard, a transplanted New Yorker, Lois H. Jones, wrote to the *Miami Herald* asking for a title based on her state of origin. The newspaper's answer was: "The usual nickname for people from New York is simply New Yorker, but if you want to get fancy, maybe you can call yourself an Imperialist, since the state is known as the Empire State." "There's just not a lot of colorful monikers you can hang on yourself," says Jean Palmer, librarian in the Local History Special Collections Department of the Onondaga County Library in New York. "Actually, New Yorkers don't go much for nicknames," she says. "That's why we're mostly called New Yorkers..." (*Miami Herald*, October 11, 1988). Historic nicknames and slang terms include *Knickerbocker*, *Excelsior* and *Nooyawker*.
COMMON NICKNAMES: The Empire State (from its commercial importance) and The Excelsior State (from the motto on its coat-of-arms).

New York, New York, USA. *New Yorker*. The names *Gothamite* and *Manhattanite* are also used.
   Derivative for that which is typical or characteristic of the city is *New Yorkiana*.
   The city is nicknamed the Big Apple, a term that etymologist David Shulman traces back to 1909, and has attracted a number

of other alternatives from O'Henry's *Yaptown-on-the-Hudson* to the fanciful *Alaspooryork,* the name that won a 1971 contest to rename the place if it seceded from the state and established itself as an independent city-state.

New Zealand. *New Zealander.* Adjective: *New Zealand.*

Niagara Falls, New York, USA. There is no commonly accepted term, but *Niagaran* has been used.

Nicaragua (Republic of Nicaragua). *Nicaraguan.* One finds the shortened *Nic* used in newspaper headlines—"U.S. pushes to expel Nic ambassador," *Boston Herald* July 14, 1988—which seems prompted by space considerations rather than an attempt to create a new term.

Niger (Republic of Niger, formerly part of French West Africa). *Nigerien,* according to the CIA's *World Factbook,* but *Webster's Ninth New Collegiate Dictionary* uses *Nigerois.*

Nigeria (Federal Republic of Nigeria). *Nigerian.*

Nile River. No commonly accepted demonym. Adjective: *Nilotic.*

Niles, Ohio, USA. *Nilesite.*

Norfolk (county), **England, UK**. *North Anglian.*

Norfolk, Nebraska, USA. *Norfolkan.*

Norfolk, Virginia, USA. *Norfolkian.*

North America. *North American.*

North Carolina (state), **USA**. *North Carolinian* or *Tar Heel* (*q.v.*). *Carolinian* is used for residents of both North and South Carolina. Historic nicknames and slang terms include *Tarboiler, Tucko* and *Turpentiner.*

COMMON NICKNAMES: Tar Heel State or Old North State (to distinguish it from South Carolina).

North Dakota (state), **USA**. *North Dakotan*, although *Dakotan* is used for residents of both North and South Dakota. On occasion, *Nodak* is used as a combination nickname/abbreviation, as is *Flickertail*. In recent years there have been several small attempts to have North Dakota renamed *Dakota*— to fight what has been termed an image of "blizzards and rocks"—but it is doubtful that anything will come of it. (Columnist George Will puckishly suggested that if the state really wanted to change its image it should re-name itself Bermuda.)
COMMON NICKNAMES: Sioux State, Flickertail State, The Peace Garden State and The Cyclone State.

Northeast, USA (The nine states making up the New England states and the Middle Atlantic states). *Northeasterner*.

Northern Ireland (A division of the United Kingdom of Great Britain and Northern Ireland). *Irish* or *Northern Irish*, but also *English*, depending on the circumstances.

Northern Rhodesia. See **Zambia**.

North Korea. *Korean*.

North Slope, Alaska, USA (A string of mountains extending across the top of the state). *North Sloper*.

Northumberland (county), England, **UK**. *Northumbrian*.

Norse. See *Norway*.

Northwest Territory (state), **Australia**. *Territorian* or *Topender*. See entry for **Banana-Bender**.

Norway (Kingdom of Norway). *Norwegian. Norse* is used as an adjective, although it is also an adjective for Scandinavian.

Norseman and *Norsewoman* are also applied to Norwegians, but are correct for any Scandinavian.

Nova Scotia (province), **Canada**. *Nova Scotian*; also the popular slang term *Bluenose*. It takes its name from an apparently superior potato of that name which was once grown there. It is also the name of a Nova Scotian sailing ship, launched in 1921, which became so famous that it was depicted on the Canadian 10-cent piece first issued in 1936.

Novocastrian.   Resident of New Castle, England, UK or New South Wales, Australia.

Nutmegger.   Resident of Connecticut.

Nyasaland. *Nyasalander* (obsolete); now Malawi.

O

Oakland, California, USA. *Oaklander*. Two negative names are *Joaklander* and *Ughlander*.

Oak Park, Illinois, USA. *Oakparker*.

Oaxaca, Mexico. *Oaxacan*.

OBtian. Resident of Ocean Beach, a section of San Diego, California. A demonymic oddity reported by OBtian Ellen Todd, who writes, "I live in the Ocean Beach section of San Diego. We all have a penchant for giving our cities and neighborhoods letter abbreviations 'LA,' 'SD,' and so on; so our community is called 'OB.' We are therefore OBtians, O-B-shuns."

Occident. *Occidental*.

Oceania (Collective name for the lands of the Central and South Pacific). *Oceanian*.

off-islander. Generic term. Expression popular on some islands for people from anywhere but the island in question. It has a strong association with the island of Nantucket because of a Nathaniel Benchley book called *The Off-Islanders*, which

was made into the movie *The Russians Are Coming! The Russians Are Coming!* In addition to applying to tourists and visitors, the term is likely to refer to a person who lives on the island (full or part time) but was not born there. Jonathan Tourtellot of the National Geographic Society reports a variation: "If you're not Manx but live on the Isle of Man, you're a 'Come-over.'"

Ohio (state), **USA**.   *Ohioan*, but the nickname *Buckeye* is sometimes used. The nickname *Yellowhammer* was once popular.
COMMON NICKNAMES: The Buckeye State, from the local name for horse chestnuts.

Okie.   Pejorative term for Oklahoman, mainly because it is so strongly tied to poor, migratory farm workers from Oklahoma. In 1947 H.L. Mencken noted that the term is "not tolerated locally, though it is in wide use elsewhere, especially in California, which received the brunt of the mass migration in 1935, described with poetic fancy in John E. Steinbeck's *Grapes of Wrath*." It seems that the term existed before Steinbeck's 1939 novel, but the migration helped spread it.

Oklahoma (state), **USA**.   *Oklahoman*, preferred to *Oklahomian*. The nickname *Sooner* (tied to the University of Oklahoma) is also used. See *Okie* for pejorative variation.
COMMON NICKNAME: Sooner State.

Oklahoma City, Oklahoma, USA.   *Oklahoma Citian*.

Old World (The eastern hemisphere comprised of China, India, Europe and Africa).   *Old Worlder*. The term is also used to refer to Europe in the sense of Old World customs.

Omaha, Nebraska, USA.   *Omahan*.

Oman (Sultanate of Oman).   *Omani*.

Ontario (province), **Canada**.   *Ontarian*.

Orcadian.   Resident of the Orkneys.

Oregon (state), **USA**.   *Oregonian*. Historic nicknames and slang terms include *Webfoot*, *Beaver* and *Hard Case*.
COMMON NICKNAMES. Beaver State, from the area's early fur trade.

Orient.   *Oriental*. Also used as an adjective in oriental cooking, and oriental rug.

Orkneys/Orkney Islands, Scotland, UK.   *Orcadian*, although *Orkneyan* is sometimes used, as in *Orkney Islander* and *Orkneyman/Orkneywoman*.

Orlando, Florida, USA.   *Orlandoan*.

Orleanian.   Archaic. Resident of New Orleans, Louisiana. See also *Orleenian*.

Orleenian.   Resident of New Orleans, although *Orleanian* is much more common.

Oshkosh, Wisconsin, USA.   This comment appeared in George R. Stewart, Jr.'s "Names for Americans" in *American Speech*, February 1934: "Oshkosh is stumped by its own name, the press there sticking to 'Oshkosh man' or 'Oshkosh woman.' The name is of Indian origin, so that 'Oshkosher' might not be kosher."

Oslo, Norway.   *Osloer*.

Ottawa, Kansas, USA.   *Ottawan*.

Ottawa, Ontario, Canada.   *Ottawan*. But also *Byetowner*, from the fact that British Army Engineer Colonel William Bye built the Rideau Canal and Trent water systems of locks and canals.

out-of-stater.   In the United States, a generic term for a tourist. It tends to be used as a term of derision. "Most of the trout fisherman were Easterners, middle-age men with money. It wasn't considered polite anymore to say 'dudes.' 'Out-of-

stater' was the currently accepted epithet" (*Incident at Big Sky* by Johnny France and Malcolm McConnell).

Oxford and Oxfordshire (county), **England, UK**. *Oxonian,* a term that also applies to a graduate of Oxford University. The journal published by the Associated of American Rhodes Scholars is *The American Oxonian. Oxfordian* is sometimes used for residents of Oxford as well as for a school of thought that ascribes the writings of Shakespeare to Edward de Vere, the 17th earl of Oxford. The *Oxford English Dictionary* lists a number of derivatives, including *Oxfordish, Oxfordian, Oxfordy* and *Oxonolatry* (for love of the place).

Oz (Fictional realm in the fantasy novels of L. Frank Baum and a nickname for Australia). *Ozzie* is used for a native of Australia. It derives from *Aussie.* The term *Oziana* is used for that which is characteristic of Oz.

Ozarks/Ozark Mountains, USA. *Ozarker.*   Adjective: *Ozarkian.*
   Historically, the area seems to have had a number of odd local nicknames designed to puzzle outsiders. A March 3, 1934 AP dispatch in the *San Francisco Call Bulletin* (Tamony Collection) attempted to sort them out: "The 'Hog Rangers' live south of the Osage River and their neighbors, the 'Elm Peelers,' live on the north side of the River. In the hunting country live the 'Rabbit Twisters,' who save ammunition by twisting a stick in the fur of rabbits in hollow logs and dragging them out. The 'Squirrel Knocks' kill their game with rocks. The 'Scissorbills' live in the valleys; the 'Ridge Runners' atop the cedar stubbed hogbacks. The 'Sprout Splitters' are in the cut over timber country."

Ozzie. See **Oz**.

P

Pakistan (Islamic Republic of Pakistan). *Pakistani*. The shortened *Pak* is also used, but the term *Paki*, as used in jokes, is clearly derogatory.

Palau (Republic of Palau, an American trust territory in the Pacific). *Palauan*.

Palestine. *Palestinian*.

Palmyra Island. *Palmyrene*.

Palois. Resident of Pau, France.

Panama (Republic of Panama). *Panamanian*.

Panama Canal Zone. *Zonian* is the term used for U.S. citizens living there.

Panama City, Panama. *Panamanian*.

Papua New Guinea. *Papua New Guinean*.

Paraguay (Republic of Paraguay). *Paraguayan*.

Paris, France. *Parisian* (male) or *Parisienne* (female).

Pasadena, California, USA. *Pasadenan.*

Patagonia, Argentina. *Patagonian.*

Paterson, New Jersey, USA. *Patersonian.*

Patrick's People. Name that the Irish have sometimes applied to themselves, a reference to St. Patrick.

Paulista. Resident of São Paulo, Brazil.

Pea Souper. Contemptuous term for a French-Canadian, derived from the diet of the voyagers in the days of the fur trade.

Pegger. Resident of Winnipeg, Canada.

Peiping, Peking or Peiking, People's Republic of China. *Pekinese.*

Pennsylvania (nominally a state, but legally a commonwealth), **USA.** *Pennsylvanian.*
   Historic nicknames and slang terms include *Coal Miner, Cohee, Iron Puddler, Leatherhead, Loggerhead, Penancer, Pennanite* and *Quaker.*
COMMON NICKNAME: Keystone State, from the time when there were 13 states and a popular wood-cut, depicted the new nation as an arch with Pennsylvanian as the keystone.

Pennsylvania Dutch. The descendants of German immigrants who cling to certain Germanic speech patterns and customs are known as the *Pennsylvanian Dutch.* The dialect is different enough that the *New York Times* could carry an item like this: "Pennsylvania State University is offering a course in 'Pennsylvania Dutch'—spoken only by 300,000 Pennsylvanians" (October 2, 1955). Briton Ross Reader writes to point out that "Pennsylvania Dutch" is a very confusing term to strangers coming to the United States.

Peoria, Illinois, USA. *Peorian.*

Persia. *Persian.* Persia is now Iran, but the term is still used as an adjective in describing such goods as Persian carpets and Persian lamb coats. The language of the Islamic Republic of Iran is *Farsi*, but some outside the country still refer to it as Persian. One name that has remained current is *Persian Gulf*, although the U.S. Department of Defense began calling it the *Arabian Gulf* in 1987.

Peru (Republic of Peru). *Peruvian.*

Petersburger. Resident of or one born in what was St. Petersburg, Russia; now Leningrad, USSR.

Philadelphia, Pennsylvania, USA. *Philadelphian.*

Philippines (Republic of the Philippines). *Filipino.* Adjective: *Philippine.*

Phoenix, Arizona, USA. *Phoenician.*

Piker. Archaic and pejorative term for Missourian. In his *Dictionary of Americanisms* (University of Chicago, 1951), M.M. Mathews suggests that it came from the days of the California Gold Rush when so many of the Missourians came from Pike County.

Piqua, Ohio, USA. *Piquard.*

Pilltowner. Resident of Hollywood, California, in the slang of the 1950s when the film colony there was building its reputation as an enormous consumer of tranquilizers. A typical *Pilltown/Pilltowner* quip of the time was this one from Earl Wilson's column (October 2, 1956): "Out in Pilltown, USA... many of the stars now have pool-shaped kidneys... "

Pitcairn Islands (A British colony with a population of 48). *Pitcairner*.

Pittsburgh, Pennsylvania, USA. *Pittsburgher* is preferred but *Pittsburger* is acceptable. The regional quirks in vocabulary and speech (rubber bands are gumbands in this town, where the sidewalks get slippy, not slippery) are lumped together under the name *Pittsburghese*. The blend name *Pittsylvania* is used to describe an area of southwestern Pennsylvania along with neighboring portions of Maryland and West Virginia, which are dominated by the city of Pittsburgh. A book entitled, *Pittsylvania Country* by George Swetnam was published in 1951.

Towns called Pittsburg (no "h") exist in California, Illinois, Kansas, New Hampshire, Oklahoma and Texas.

Plymouth, Massachusetts, USA. *Plymouthian*. A bumper sticker spotted in that town on May 11, 1988 alluded to its recent development: NATIVE PLYMOUTHIAN—AN ENDANGERED SPECIES.

podunk. Generic term. For generations, a hick town inhabited by boors, rubes and *Podunkers*. Several real Podunks exist, including a sparsely settled section of East Brookfield, Massachusetts; and the town of Podunk Center, Iowa, which was offered for sale in 1969 for $7,000 (at which time it had no population).

Poland (Polish People's Republic). *Pole*. Adjective: *Polish*.

Pomponian. Resident of Portsmouth, Hampshire, which is known as Pompey in the British navy. Phillip Chaplin of Ottawa who was once home-ported there in the navy reports that the traditional name for him and his mates was the Pompey ratings.

Pooshtoonistan (A short-lived nation on Afghanistan's eastern border that proclaimed its independence on November 20, 1949). *Pooshtoonistani*.

Porkopolitan. Resident of Cincinnati from the time when the city processed hogs and it was known as *Porkopolis*.

Porteño. Resident of Bueños Aires, Argentina.

Portland, Maine and Portland, Oregon, USA. *Portlander*.

Portsmouth, Hampshire, England, UK. *Pomponian*.
Portsmouth is known as Pompey in the British navy.

Portsmouth, Ohio, New Hampshire and Virginia, USA.
Portsmouthite.

Portugal (Portuguese Republic). *Portuguese* (both singular
and plural). See **Lusitania**.

Prague, Czechoslovakia. *Praguer* or *Prazan* (Czech.)

Prince Edward Island (province), **Canada**. *Spud Islander*
(slang but common). It comes from the fact that the tiny
province exports potatoes. Also *Islander* and *Prince Edward
Islander*.

Princeton, New Jersey, USA. *Princetonian*, which is also used
to describe the students and graduates of Princeton University.

Proper Bostonian. *Brahmin*.

Providence, Rhode Island, USA. *Providentian*, although
many residents of the city seem content to be called *Rhode
Islander* instead.

Puerto Rico *Puerto Rican* is the common term, but the Spanish
Puertorriqueños is appearing in more and more English-lan-
guage publications. A much less common term is *Borinquen*,
after the name of the Indian tribe of the island at the time of the
arrival of Columbus. See entry for **Neorican**.

Puke. Derogatory nickname for Missourian that was common
before World War I at a time when Illinoisans were known as
Suckers and the term *Hoosier* has a rougher edge to it. Peter
Tamony toyed with two possible origins for the term: (1) that

it is a mispronunciation of the Pike of Pike County and/or (2) that it came about during a lead-mine boom in Illinois in 1827 that inspired the Suckers to say that Missouri had "taken a puke," that it had vomited up its people. Another notion suggests itself in the writing of Davy Crockett in his 1835 *Almanac of Wild Sports of the West, and Life in the Backwoods,* in which he gives a long and highly incendiary definition of the Missouri *Puke,* emphasizing extreme ugliness. Consequently, wrote Crockett, "The Pukes never look each other in the face but once a year, an' that's in the spring, when they want to vomit off their surplus bile."

Purdulian. Person associated with Purdue University, Indiana.

Q

Qatar (State of Qatar). *Qatari.*

Quebec or Québec (province), **Canada**. *Québecker, Québecer* or *Québecois*. The "ck" version has largely eclipsed the second spelling in written English. This may have stemmed from the fact that René Lévesque, the leader of the 1970s who worked to have that province secede, let it be known that he preferred *Québecker. Québecois* (Kaybeckwah) is used in both French and English for a francophone resident of the province. The *New York Times Manual of Style and Usage* calls for *Québecer* in news stories but adds that "*Québecois* (sing. and pl.) may be used in references to the distinctive French-Canadian culture of Québec; a Québecois novelist or, "Above all," the separatist leader said, "I am proud to be be Québecois." The term *Parti Québecois* is an exception to the general rule followed by the *Times* and other newspapers, which is to translate the name of foreign political parties. (Interestingly, *Times* language columnist William Safire opposed this exception writing, "If we're going to speak English, let's put it in English."

Queensland (state), **Australia**. *Queenslander* or *Banana-Bender* (*q.v.*).

Queutopia. See entry for *Utopian*.

Quincy, Illinois, USA. *Quincyan*.

Quito, Ecuador. *Quiteño*.

R

Ra's al-Khaymah (One of the United Arab Emirates). *Emirian*.

Razorback. Nickname for the University of Arkansas that is sometimes applied to the residents of the state. The razorback is a wild hog. In another incarnation the *razorback* show up as a slang for a circus or carnival laborer.

Redneck/Red Neck/Red-Neck. Term for a rural, Southern (U.S.) white who is usually poor and has presumably reddened the back of his neck working in the fields. In most contexts it is a term of derogation but can be used as a self-described badge of pride.

The term has been around for some time. Peter Tamony found this in the writings of George Ade: "Every time I see him over at the City Hall he's whisperin' to one of them red-necked boys and fixin' it up to give somebody the double-cross" (*Artie*, 1896). By the 1930s the term was in use as a term in news accounts of elections to describe the untutored, bigoted segment of the electorate: "It soon became apparent to Theodore Bilbo that his camp-meeting rabble-rousing rant had a definite appeal for rural 'red-necks'" (*Time*, October 1, 1934).

Despite this, the term was once used by trade unionists as a synonym for the slang "roughneck"—a tough, hard worker.

Regiomontaño.   Resident of Monterrey, Mexico.

resident.   Generic term. Person living in a place. As states and cities cannot grant citizenship, *The Associated Press Stylebook and Libel Manual* holds that one can be a *citizen* of the United States but a *resident* of Oklahoma, e.g.

Reno, Nevada, USA.   *Renoite*. Nevadan Robert J. Throckmorton is not the first to point out that this demonym looks clumsy in print: "When I first saw it, I wondered what a 'Ree-noit-ee' was."

Réunion (French Overseas Department of Réunion).   *Réunionese* (both singular and plural) is preferred by the CIA's *World Factbook*. However *Réunionais* is used by those who prefer to keep closer to the French. It is located to the east of Madagascar in the Indian Ocean.

Rhinelander.   Resident of the Rhine Valley region of Germany, but sometimes erroneously applied to any German. It has also been used to describe Cincinnati because of its heavy concentration of German immigrants. The term is used less and less today, b ut as recently as 1959 the report of a baseball game form the city began like this: "It's like old times here in the Rhineland. Willie Mays still is the favorite 'brush-ball' target of the Redleg pitchers" (*San Francisco News*, May 5, 1959, PT).

Rhode Island (state), **USA**.   *Rhode Islander*. *Gun Flint* is a nickname that shows up in slang collections but is little used, if at all, today. *Rhodian* as an R.I. adjective shows up in print as early as 1722 when a poet was called "a Rhodian muse" in the *New England Courant*.
COMMON NICKNAMES: Little Rhody and The Ocean State.

Rhodesia.   *Rhodesian* (obsolete); now Zimbabwe. The derivative nickname "*Rhodie*," after the former name of the country, is in current use for the nation's 20,000 white *Zimbabweans*.

Richmond, California and Indiana, USA.   *Richmondite*.

Richmond, Virginia, USA. *Richmonder.*

Rio de Janeiro, Brazil. *Carioca.*

Rio Muni. See **Equatorial Guinea.**

Rochester, Indiana, USA. *Rochesterite.*

Rochester, New York, USA. *Rochesterian.*

Rockford, Illinois, USA. There is no commonly accepted term in use, but *Rockfordian* could be used in a pinch.

Roman. Resident of Rome, Italy; also used in references to ancient Rome.

Romania (Socialist Republic of Romania). *Romanian.* Sometimes these terms are spelled with a u to form Rumania and *Roumanian.*

Rome, Italy. *Roman.*

Roosky/Ruskie and Russky. Cold War-era nicknames for the Russian people. Clearly a term of mild defamation along the lines of calling a Communist a Commie; however, they are sometimes used with some affection. News accounts of the meeting of American and Russian troops at the Elbe River in 1945 told of GIs putting their arms around Soviet troops and calling them "Russkys" (Associated Press dispatch of May 4, 1945).

Russia (The Russian Soviet Federated Socialist Republic). *Russian.* Specifically, person from one of the 15 republics comprising the Union of Soviet Socialist Republics. *The Associated Press Stylebook and Libel Manual* points out that Russia dominates the other 14 republics and *Russia, Russian* and *Russians* are acceptable synonyms for Soviet Union, Soviet and *Soviets* when talking about the government apparatus, such as "Russians to begin new round of missile reduction talks."

However, Russia and its derivatives are not appropriate for references to all the people of the Soviet Union. See *Roosky*, *Ruskie* and *Russky* for derogatory nicknames.

Rust Belt/Rust-Belt/Rustbelt (Collective term for the older industrial states of the U.S. Northeast and Middle West). No name has emerged for a resident (Rustbelter is simply too awkward and confusing), but rust belt exists as an adjective: "Rust Belt Resurgence" (*Tampa Tribune*, April 7, 1988) and "A Rust-Belt Relic's New Shine" (*Newsweek*, September 9, 1985). See *Sunbelt*.

Rutland, Vermont, USA. *Rutlander.*

Rwanda (Republic of Rwanda, formerly part of U.N. Trustee Territory of Ruanda-Urundi). *Rwandan,* according to the CIA's *World Factbook*, but *Rwandese* appears in print.

Ryukyu Archipelago (Islands in the Pacific, south of Japan). *Ryukyuan.*

S

Sacramento, California, USA. *Sacramentan.*

Sagebrusher. Nickname used by a person in the rural U.S. West to describe himself or herself.

Saigon, Vietnam. There is no commonly accepted term in use, as the custom is to refer to residents of that city as Vietnamese (See entry for **Bangkok** for a discussion of a similar case)

Saint Christopher and Nevis (Federation of Saint Christopher and Nevis). *Kittsian* and *Nevisian.* This Caribbean nation is also known as St. Kitts-Nevis. See also *Anguilla.*

Saint-Cloud, France. *Clodoaldien* (male), *Clodoaldienne* (female).

Saint Croix, Virgin Islands. *Cruzan.*

Saint-Dié, France. *Déodatien* (male), *Déodatienne* (female).

Saint-Dizier, France. *Bragard* (male), *Bragarde* (female).

Sainte-Foy, Quebec, Canada. *Fidéen.*

Saint Grottlesexer. Term used to designate students and graduates of a group of elite Northeastern prep schools with church affiliations. The schools covered collectively by the term are Groton, St. Mark's, St. Paul's, St. George's and Middlesex.

Saint John, New Brunswick, Canada. *Saint Johner,* but pronounced "Sinjohnner" according to a Canadian source, who says that the term is useful in distinguishing the Saint Johnners from their counterparts in St. John's, Newfoundland, who are known as "Noofi-johnners."

Saint John's, Newfoundland, Canada. *St. Johnsians,* but as Alan Rayburn pointed out in *Canadian Geographic* "...they are really better known as 'townies', as opposed to 'baymen' who live in outpost communities."

Saint Kitts-Nevis. See **Saint Christopher and Nevis.**

Saint Louis, Missouri, USA. *Saint Louisan.*

Saint Lucia. *Saint Lucian.*

Saint-Malo, France. *Malouin* (male), *Malouine* (female).

Saint Paul, Minnesota, USA. *Saint Paulite.*

Saint-Paul-Trois-Chateaux, France. *Tricastin* or *Tricastinois.*

Saint Petersburg, Florida, USA. *Saint Petersburgite* appears correct, but bulky. Locally, people seem to be described as a *St. Pete man* or *St. Pete woman.*

Saint-Valéry-en-Caux, France. *Valéricais.*

Saint-Valéry-sur-Somme, France. *Valéricain.*

Saint Vincent and the Grenadines. *St. Vincentian* or *Vincentian.*

Salem, Massachusetts, New Jersey and Oregon, USA.   *Salemite.*

Salina, Kansas, USA. *Salinan.*

Salinas, California, USA. *Salinan.*

Salopian.   Resident of Shropshire, England.

Salt Lake City, Utah, USA. *Salt Laker.*

Salvadoran.   Resident of El Salvador. Researcher Charles Poe has found the variant *Salvadorian* in print, but it appears to lack widespread support. Also, *Salvadorean.*

Samoa. *Samoan.* A resident of American Samoa is known simply as a *Samoan*, but a resident of Western Samoa is sometimes referred to as a *Western Samoan.*

San Antonio, Texas, USA. *San Antonian.*

Sand-groper.   Resident of west Australia. See entry for **Banana-Bender.**

San Diego, California, USA. *San Diegan.*

San Francisco, California, USA. *San Franciscan.* Because this city is unlike the cities to the south (notably Los Angeles and San Diego), there are those who have parroted horesman Harry McCarty's line: "I am not a Californian, I am a San Franciscan." See entry for **Friscan.**

San Jose, California, USA. *San Josean.*

San Juan, Puerto Rico, USA. *San Juanero.*

Sanmarinese.   Resident of San Marino.

San Marino (The Most Serene Republic of San Marino). *Sanmarinese* (both singular and plural).

Santa Ana, California, USA. *Santa Anan.*

Santa Barbara, California, USA. *Barbareno, Santa Barbareno* or *Santa Barbaran.*

Santa Fe, New Mexico, USA. *Santa Fean.*

Santiago, Chile. *Santiaguiño.*

São Paulo, Brazil. *Paulista.*

São Tomé and Príncipe (Democratic Republic of São Tomé and Príncipe). *São Tomean.*

Sardinia, Italy. *Sardinian.*

Saskatchewan (province), **Canada.** *Saskatchewaner* or *Saskatchewanian.*

Saskatoon, Saskatchewan, Canada. *Saskatooner,* or *Saskatonian.*

Saturn (planet). *Saturnian.*

Saudi Arabia (Kingdom of Saudi Arabia). *Saudi.* Adjective: *Saudi Arabian* or *Saudi.*

Saugus, Massachusetts, USA. *Saugonian.*

Savannah, Georgia, USA. *Savannahian.*

Scandinavia (Collective name for the territory containing Sweden, Denmark, Norway and Finland). *Scandinavian*   or *Norse.* The latter can be confusing as it is also used as an adjective to refer to Norway. *Scandahoovian/Scandinovi-*

an/Scoovian are playful nicknames likely to show up in a humourous context. Evidence in the Tamony Collection suggests that these names may have first shown up in the Minnesota humor magazine *Capt. Billy's Whiz Bang* in the 1920s. *Skijumper* is still another nickname but has not been popular for many years.

Schenectady, New York, USA. *Schenectadian*. Geof Huth of Schenectady reports that the city is often referred to as *Dorp*—making a citizen a *Dorpian*—which he adds is a blessing to headline writers.

The term obviously fascinated H. L. Mencken, who wrote about it in his February 8, 1936 article on "municipal onomastics" in the *New Yorker*: "A citizen of Schenectady, New York, will answer sheepishly to the name *Schenectadian*, but he greatly prefers *Dorpian* from the ancient Dutch designation of the town—the *Dorp*, or the *Old Dorp*."

Dorp is the Dutch word for "village."

Scotland. *Scot, Scotsman/Scotswoman* or *Scotchman/Scotchwoman* are all used commonly. Adjectives: *Scots*, *Scottish* and *Scotch*. These seem ordained by tradition: Scotch whiskey, the Scottish dialect, Scotch broth, etc.

In attempting to deal with this "vexed question," Robert W. Chapman wrote in his *Adjectives for Proper Names*, "These variations should be received as a compliment to the national versatility."

Scouse or Scouser. Resident of Liverpool, England; lower-class usage.

Scranton, Pennsylvania, USA. *Scrantonian*.

Seattle, Washington, USA. *Seattleite*.

Senegal (Republic of Senegal, formerly part of French West Africa). *Senegalese* (both singular and plural).

Seychelles (Republic of Seychelles). *Seychellois* (both singular and plural). Adjective: *Seychelles*.

Shanghai, People's Republic of China. *Shanghailander,* or *Shanghainese.*

Shanty Irish. Poor Irish, specifically people who lived in mean huts in their home country and came to the United States after the potato famine of 1846. The term distinguishes them from the middle-class, or *Lace Curtain Irish.*

Sharjah (One of the United Arab Emirates). *Emirian.*

Shreveport, Louisiana, USA. *Shreveporter.*

Shropshire, England, UK. *Salopian.*

Siberia, USSR. *Siberian.* An extremely cold weather system coming out of Siberia into North America has been termed a "Siberian Express."

Sicily, Italy. *Sicilian.*

Sierra Leone. *Sierra Leonean.*

Silver Stater. Resident of Nevada, the Silver State. *Nevadan,* however, is much more common.

Singapore (Republic of Singapore). *Singaporean.* Adjective: *Singapore.* (Washingtonian Tim Gibson recalls a classic demonymic misnomer at a racetrack's International Day during which an entry from Singapore was referred to as a *Singapese* horse.)

Sioux Falls, South Dakota, USA. This is a difficult case prompting Bill McKean of Sioux Falls to write: "People from Sioux Falls are called PEOPLE FROM SIOUX FALLS. There are limits." There is at least one alternative; however: *Siouxlander,* for a person living along the Big Sioux River, including people from Sioux Falls. A note from Michael McDonald of Hudson, South Dakota, explains, "A number of residents of Sioux Falls, S.D., have adopted the term Frederick Manfred gave to the residents who live along the Big Sioux River and call themselves Siouxlanders. However, a Siouxlander includes Sioux Citians, Cantonites, Hudsonites, etc. who also have ties to the river."

Slovak. Person from the eastern part of Czechoslovakia (or Czecho-Slovakia as it is written by Slovaks in other parts of the world who favor its independence). They have a distinct identity (language, culture, history, etc.) that sets them apart from the Czechs.

Smogvillian. Comic name for resident of Los Angeles, based on its characteristic smog. In the same vein, when the Brooklyn Dodgers became the Los Angeles Dodgers, several newspaper columnists suggested that they be called the *Smogers*.

Solomon Islands. *Solomon Islander*.

Somalia (Somali Democratic Republic, formerly the British Protectorate of Somaliland and the Italian International Trust Territory of Somalia). *Somali*. Charles Poe's research revealed an example of *Somalians* ("Somalians fleeing," headline in the *Houston Post*, July 3, 1988), but it seems to be an aberration and without support as an alternative to *Somali*.

Sooner. Nickname for the University of Oklahoma as well as for an *Oklahoman*. The name goes back to the opening of the Oklahoma Territory in 1889. The lands were vacant and were to be opened legally for settlement at noon on April 22, 1889. Some sneaked in before the official time and were immediately dubbed "sooners."

(*Sooner* has also seen some slang use for a child born less than nine months after the parents' wedding.)

South, USA. *Southerner*.

South Africa (Republic of South Africa). *South African*.

South America. *South American*.

South Australia (state), **Australia**. *South Australian* or *Crow-Eater*. See entry for *Banana-Bender* to understand how this nickname can be defamatory.

South Bend, Indiana, USA. *South Bender*.

South Carolina (state), **USA**. *South Carolinian*. *Carolinian* is used for residents of both North and South Carolina. Historic nicknames and slang terms include *Clay Eater*, *Palmetto*, *Ricebird*, *Sandlapper* and *Weasel*.
COMMON NICKNAME: Palmetto State, because its coat-of-arms features a palmetto tree.

South Dakota (state), **USA**. *South Dakotan*. *Dakotan* is used for residents of both North and South Dakota. An oddity here was a weekly newspaper established in the 1880s entitled *Conklin's South Dakotian*.
COMMON NICKNAMES: Sunshine State, Coyote State and The Blizzard State.

Southeast Asia. (Collective name for the nations of the In-dochinese peninsula: Myanma (Burma), Cambodia, Indonesia, Laos, Malaysia, Papua, New Guinea, the Philippines, Sin-gapore, Thailand and Vietnam.) *Southeast Asian*.

South Korea. *Korean* or *South Korean*.

Soviet Union (Union of Soviet Socialist Republics). *Soviet*.

Soweto, South Africa. *Sowetan*. The name is also that of a black newspaper that serves the sprawling black township.

Spain. *Spaniard*.

Spaniard. Resident of Spain.

Sparnacien/Sparnacienne. Resident of Épernay, France.

Spinalien/Spinalienne. Resident of Épinal, France.

Spokane, Washington, USA. *Spokanite.*

Springfield, Illinois, USA. *Springfielder* or *Springfieldman/-Springfieldwoman.*

Spud/Spud Islander. Resident of Prince Edward Island, Canada. See **Prince Edward Island**.

Sri Lanka (Democratic Socialist Republic of Sri Lanka, formerly Ceylon). *Sri Lankan*, although *Ceylonese* is sometimes still used.

State-of-Mainer. One of several names for a resident of Maine. Curiously, it is the lone example of a demonym using the words "state of."

Stockholm, Sweden. *Stockholmer*. Adjective: *Stockholmian.*

Storrs, Connecticut, USA *Storrsian.*

Stratford-on-Avon, England, UK. *Stratfordian*. The term is also used as a label for those who defend William Shakespeare as the author of his own plays, as opposed to, say, those who argue that the bard was Edward de Vere, the 17th earl of Oxford. See **Oxford**.

subject. Generic term. Person ruled by a monarch or other sovereign.

suburbia. Generic term. *Suburbanite*. A number of mocking synonyms having been created for this realm between the city and the country, among them, the *snuburbs* and the *shruburbs*. Commenting on the drinking observed on commuter trains, the later Walter Winchell called them *subourbonites*. Aphorist Arthur Brisbane typified them as a "…graveyard with modern plumbing."

Sudan (Democratic Republic of the Sudan). *Sudanese* (both singular and plural).

Sumatra. *Sumatran*.

Sun Belt/Sunbelt (Collective term for the warm states of the South and Southwest, U.S.).   No name has emerged for a resident (Sunbelter has attracted little enthusiasm), but Sun Belt exists as an adjective: e.g., "Sun Belt migration." See also *Rustbelt*.

Suriname (Republic of Suriname).   *Surinamer*. Adjective: *Surinamese*.

Swaziland (Kingdom of Swaziland).   *Swazi*.

Sweden (Kingdom of Sweden).   *Swede*. Adjective: *Swedish*.

Switzerland (Swiss Confederation).   *Swiss* (both singular and plural).

Sydney, New South Wales, Australia. *Sydneysider* or *Sydneyite*. The former term is used for the city as well as the neighboring area of New South Wales, of which Sydney is the capital.

Syracuse, New York, USA.   Syracusan. It is also applied to the residents of ancient Syracuse, although Shakespeare used *Syracusian* to refer to the people of that city.

Syria (Syrian Arab Republic).   *Syrian*.

Szechwan (province), **China.**   *Szechwanese*.

T

Tacoma, Washington, USA. *Tacoman.*

Tadzhik Soviet Socialist Republic or Tadzhikistan (Constituent Republic of the Union of Soviet Socialist Republics). *Tad-zhik* or *Tajik.*

Tahiti. *Tahitian.*

Taiwan (The Republic of China). *Taiwanian* or *Taiwanese.* The name *Formosan* is discussed under **Formosa.**

Tampa, Florida, USA. *Tampan.*

Tanganyika. *Tanganyikan.* Obsolete, as the country ceased to exist in 1964 when it merged with Zanzibar. See **Tanzania.**

Tangier, Morocco (Formerly International Zone of Tangier). *Tangerine,* also the source for the name of the fruit.

Tanzania (The United Republic of Tanzania, formerly Tanganyika and Zanzibar). (The new name was formed from the original names when the two countries merged in 1964). *Tanzanian.*

Tar Heel/Tarheel.   Resident of North Carolina, also known as *North Carolinian*, as well as the nickname for those associated with the University of North Carolina. Once a term of derogation, it has long since become honorific—for instance, the *Raleigh News and Observer* runs a regular feature on prominent citizens called "The Tar Heel of the Week." William S. Powell writes in the March 1982 issue of the university's *Tar Heel* magazine, "North Carolina residents have taken an albatross from around their necks and pinned it on their chests like a badge of honor."

It comes from the tar and pitch produced by the state's pine forests. As a colony, North Carolina produced tar for the British navy, exporting some 100,000 barrels of tar and pitch to England in the years just before the American Revolution.

Also used as an adjective, as in "Clashing Styles Mark Tarheel Race" (article title in *Insight*, May 5, 1986).

Tasmania (state), **Australia.** *Tasmanian*; also *Taswegian*, as well as the puckish*Tasmaniac*.

Taswegian.   Resident of Tasmania (state), Australia.

Tehran, Iran. *Tehrani*.

Tenderfoot.   Historical term for an Easterner (U.S.) gone west; a greenhorn.

Tennessee (state), **USA.** *Tennessean* is preferred over the rare and awkward *Tennesseean*. Historic nicknames and slang terms include *Big Bender, Butternut, Cotton-Mainie, Hardhead, Mudhead* and *Whelp*.
COMMON NICKNAME: Volunteer State.

Territorian.   Resident of the Northern Territory, Australia.

Texas (state), **USA.** *Texan*. The term *Texian* has a long and distinguished history but is becoming increasingly archaic. As recently as 1951 one finds a book review (of Frank X. Tolbert's

Informal History of Texas) in which the word *Texian* appears four times, but *Texan* is never mentioned. (August 4, 1961, *San Francisco Chronicle*, Peter Tamony). Texas-born writer Joseph C. Goulden reports on *Texian*: "My father used this term for the name of his bookstore in Marshall, from the late 1950's until his death in 1972. The printer delivered his first batch of 5,000 envelopes and letterheads with the remark, 'Mr. Joe, I cleaned up yo' spelling.' He did a reprint with a mutter and a protest." Another term that shows up that is clearly a blend of Texan + Mexican is *Texican*, which, among other things, was the name of a 1966 western movie staring Audie Murphy.

A letter from Ralph D. Copeland of Bellaire, Texas, reports on the traditional distinctions between the various demonyms: "Here in Texas…generations of schoolchildren have been led to believe that the name for an inhabitant of the State of Coahuila and Texas—that is, a citizen before the Alamo and the battle of San Jacinto led to Texas' independence—was a Texican. Someone resident in the state between 1836 and 1845, while we were a Republic, was entitled to be known as a Texian. It was only those latecomers who arrived after we became part of the U.S. proper…who were to be called Texans."

Texan C. F. Eckhardt, who holds that the term *Texan* did not actually emerge until after the Civil War, charts the etymology of the change from *Texican* to *Texian* to *Texan*. "The original self-name for the Anglo-American settlers was Texican— Americans in Texas who didn't quite consider themselves Mexicans; though they were living in Mexican territory and holding Mexican citizenship. Following the revolution in 1936 the 'c' was dropped and 'Texicans' became 'Texians.' After the war, with the influx of Yankee carpetbaggers and similar vermin, the 'i' was assaulted by what the *Texas Almanac* called 'that harsh and unpleasant name, 'Texan.'"

Eckhardt adds that there are two special cases: *Tejanos* and *Texaners*. "*Tejanos* (pronounce it Tay-HAHN-ohs) are descended from Spanish and Spanish-Mexican families who were here before 1836." As for the latter, *Texaners* are Texas Germans.

Texas is used playfully as an adjective in describing excess or bigness. A Rolex watch is known as a "Texas Timex." That which is characteristic of the state is *Texana* and the blend of Lone Star and Mexican cooking is *Tex-Mex*.

Historic nicknames and slang terms include *Beefhead*, *Boll Weevil*, *Cowboy*, *Longhorn* and *Ranger*. A common nickname for an individual from Texas is *Tex*.
COMMON NICKNAME: Lone Star State.

Texican.   Historically, a Texas-Mexican; see **Texas**.

Thailand (Kingdom of Thailand).   *Thai*.

Third World.   *Third Worlder*. The term Third World describes underdeveloped or emerging nations. Most Third World nations are in Africa and Asia. The term distinguishes these countries from more developed ones and also implies their independence from the "free world" and the "communist world."

Tinseltown.   Nickname for Hollywood, California.

Tirol/Tyrol, Austria.   *Tirolian* or *Tyrolean*.

Tobago.   *Tobagonian*. See Trinidad and Togabo.

Togo (Republic of Togo).   *Togolese*.

Tokyo, Japan.   *Tokyoite*.

Toledo, Ohio, USA.   *Toledan*.

Tonga (Kingdom of Tonga).   *Tongan*.

Topeka, Kansas, USA.   *Topekan*.

Top-ender.   Nickname for resident of Northern Territory, Australia. See entry for ***Banana-Bender***.

Toronto, Ontario, Canada.   *Torontian*.
An unflattering reference is *Hog* or *Hogtowner*, which derives from the uncomplimentary *Hogtown* for Toronto. According to

Columbo's Canadian References, "Its origin and meaning—whether it refers to hogs or 'hogging' the wealth of Canada—are not known."

Torrance, California, USA. *Torrancite.*

Transjordan. *Transjordanian* (obsolete, as the kingdom became Jordan in 1948).

Transkei (Independent bantu [territory] South Africa). *Transkeian.*

Trenton, New Jersey, USA. *Trentonian*, which is also the name of the city's newspaper.

Tricastin or *Tricastinois*. Resident of Saint-Paul-Trois-Châteaux, France.

Trinidad and Tobago (Republic of Trinidad and Tobago). *Trinidadian* and *Tobagoan.*

Trois-Rivières, Quebec, Canada. *Trifluvien.*

Tresifleuvian. Resident of Trois-Rivières, Quebec, Canada.

Trojan. Resident of Troy, N.Y., and other Troys, ancient and modern.

Troy, New York, USA. *Trojan*. (Applies to all Troys.)

Tucson, Arizona, USA. *Tucsonan*. One *Tucsonan*, R.M. Gagliano, writes to say, "Fellow residents of Tucson may be officially known as Tucsonans, but we *true* desert rats prefer *Puebloids.*"

Tulsa, Oklahoma, USA. *Tulsan.*

Tunisia (Republic of Tunisia). *Tunisian.*

Turkey (Republic of Turkey).   *Turk.* Adjective: *Turkish.*

Turkmen Soviet Socialist Republic (Constituent Republic of the Union of Soviet Socialist Republics).   *Turkman/Turkwoman;* also, *Turkoman.*

Tuvalu (Formerly Ellice Islands).   *Tuvaluan.*

Tynesider.   Resident of Newcastle-upon-Tyne, England; also known as a *Geordie.*

Tyrol.   *Tyrolean.* See also **Tirol/Tyrol**.

U

Uganda (Republic of Uganda). *Ugandan*.

Ukrainian Soviet Socialist Republic (Constituent Republic of the Union of Soviet Socialist Republics). *Ukrainian*.

Ulster (Region of Ireland comprising Northern Ireland). *Ulsterman/Ulsterwoman* or *Ulsterite*.

Umm al-Qaywayn (One of the United Arab Emirates). *Emirian*.

Union of Soviet Socialist Republics (Soviet Union). *Russian* or *Soviet*.

United Arab Emirates. *Emirian*.

United Arab Republic. *Egyptian*.

United Kingdom (United Kingdom of Great Britain and Northern Ireland). *Briton, Englishman/Englishwoman*. The collective plural is *British*, as is the adjective.

United States/United States of America. American, a name that has historically rankled Latin Americans and Canadians. In *The American Language*, H. L. Mencken points out that many other alternatives have been proposed—*Unisian*, *Unitedstatesians*, *Columbards*, etc.—but none have stuck. Other attempts have included *Uessian*, *United Statesard*, *United Stateser*, *Unitedstatesman*, *Usanian*, *U.S.-ian* and *Saxoamericano*, the creation of a Columbian essayist who hoped to distinguish North Americans from Latin Americans. When William Safire used his popular *New York Times* "On Language" column to solicit a new crop of suggestions, his readers came up with terms like *Usatian*, *Usonan*, *Usofan*, *Us'n*, *USAmerican*, *Ussie*, *Usam*, *Statesider* and *United*. Adjectives: *American*, *U.S.*, *U.S.A.* and *United States*. See *Yankee*. See also, *America*, *Usonia*.

Upper Volta (Republic of Upper Volta, formerly part of French West Africa). *Upper Voltan*, according to the CIA's *World Factbook*, but others have used *Upper Voltese*. Adjective: *Voltaic*. All are obsolete because the country is now known as Burkina Faso.

urban. Generic term. *Urbanite* for resident of a city.

Uruguay (Oriental or Eastern Republic of Uruguay). *Uruguayan*.

Usonia. Name for a future Utopian America populated by *Usonians*. The name was borrowed from Samuel Butler by architect Frank Lloyd Wright, who used it to describe his perfect house, "The Usonia."

Utah (state), **USA**. *Utahn*, not Utaan or Utahan. This is one of those terms which is guarded with some fervor by residents of the state. When the GPO Style Board ruled in favor of *Utahan*, it was forced to reverse itself in favor of *Utahn* after getting angry letters from Senator Jake Garn (R.-Utah) and dozens of other *Utahns*.
COMMON NICKNAMES: Beehive State and The Mormon State.

Utica, New York, USA. *Utican.*

utopia. Generic term. Ideal nation or society. From Sir Thomas More's *Utopia* of 1516. Those who believe in or would inhabit such a state are known as *Utopians.*

There have been a number of plays on the term, including Winston Churchill's *Queutopia* to describe the "Utopia of Socialists," a salient characteristic of which will be long lines (queues), and *utopiate* (utopia + opiate) for a drug that brings thoughts of a Utopian existence.

Uzbek/Uzbec Soviet Socialist Republic (Constituent Republic of the Union of Soviet Socialist Republics). *Uzbek/Uzbec.*

V

Valéricain/Valéricaine. Resident of Saint-Valéry-sur-Somme, France.

Valéricais/Valéricaise. Resident of Saint-Valéry-en-Caux, France.

Vanuatu (Republic of Vanuatu, formerly the New Hebrides). *Vanuatuan.*

Vancouver, British Columbia, Canada. *Vancouverite.*

Vatican City (State of Vatican City). *Vatacanian.*

Vegas. Nickname for Las Vegas, Nevada.

Venezuela (Republic of Venezuela). *Venezuelan.*
   Venezuela is interesting in that it is a derivative of Venice. When the explorers Ojeda and Vespucci arrived at Lake Maracaibo in 1499 they found an Indian village built over the lake on pilings. They likened it to the famed Italian lagoon city and called it Venezuela, or "little Venice."

Venice, Italy. Venetian, a term that gets must adjectival application: Venetian glass, Venetian blinds, etc.

Venus (Planet). *Cytherean.* It came into prominence when the first probes were made of Venus in the late 1960s and astronomers shied away from the local choice of *venereal*, which was too closely associated with human sexual activity. The next logical choice was the Greek *aphrodisian*, which had similar sexual overtones. The final choice of *Cytherean* came from the island of Cythera, from which Aphrodite emerged. Similarly, Carl Sagan related in an article in the *New York Times* that it had been suggested that a Martian volcano be named *Mons Verenis* until he pointed out that it "had been pre-empted by quite a different field of human activity." Despite the preference for *Cytherean, The Associated Press Stylebook and Libel Manual* lists *venusian*.

Veracruz, Mexico. *Jarochos.*

Verdian. Term sometimes used for resident of Cape Verde. It can lead to confusion as the same term is used for admirers of or characteristic of Guiseppi Verdi.

Vermont (state), **USA.** *Vermonter.* As with other New England demonyms this one is not bestowed on a person when he or she arrives in the state. Michael A. Stackpole, who grew up in Vermont and now lives in Phoenix, Arizona, points out with some exaggeration that, "there's a rather strict set of rules as to who has earned that title. A Vermonter is someone born in Vermont whose parents and grandparents were also born in the state. As some of us were told when we protested (I was born in Wisconsin), 'If you were baking cookies and a puppy crawled into the oven, you wouldn't call it a 'cookie' would you?' Delivered with the proper Vermont accent it makes sense. The rest of us are 'Summer Folk' or, if we stick around for years, 'Year-round Summer Folk.'"

Historic nicknames and slang terms include *Green Mountain Boy/Girl.*
COMMON NICKNAME: The Green Mountain State.

Verona, Italy. *Veronese.*

Victoria (state), **Australia.** *Victorian* or *Cabbage-patcher.* See entry for *Banana-Bender.*

Vienna, Austria. *Viennese.* Adjective: *Viennese* and *Vienna* as in *Vienna* bread, *Vienna* sausage, etc.

Vietnam (Socialist Republic of Vietnam). *Vietnamese.*

Vincentian. Resident of Saint Vincent and the Grenadines.

Vineyarder. Resident of Martha's Vineyard, Massachusetts.

Virginia (nominally a state but legally a commonwealth), **USA**. *Virginian.* Since Virginia is known as the Old Dominion, its residents are sometimes referred to as *Dominionites.* Historic nicknames and slang terms include *Cavalier, Buckskin, Beagle, Soreback* and *Tuckahoe.*
COMMON NICKNAMES: The Old Dominion, The Mother of Presidents (seven) and The Mother of States.

Virgin Islands. *Virgin Islander* is used in both the United States and the British Virgin Islands.

W

Waco, Texas, USA. *Wacoites.* However, Texan C.F. Eckhardt of Seguin adds, "Anyone from Waco is usually called a Baptist, regardless of his/her actual religious affiliation, since Waco is home to Baylor University, which is sometimes called the 'World's Largest Baptist Preacher Factory.'"

Wales. *Welshman/Welshwoman.* Adjective: *Welsh,* as in Welsh rarebit. There has always been some confusion between *Welsh* and the slang verb to *welsh* or *welch*: to fail to meet an obligation, to run out on a debt, to betray a confidence. One theory is that it came from an old nursery rhyme with the lines, "Taffy was a Welshman, Taffy was a thief," but it seems far more likely to come from the German *welsch,* which in criminal argot meant "foreigner" and, eventually, one who did not obey the conventional rules of gambling.

Wallis and Futuna (French Overseas Territory of the Wallis and Futuna Islands). *Wallisian, Futunan* or *Wallis and Futuna Islander.*

Wash-ashore/Washashore. Traditional name given by native Cape Codders to "someone who came over the bridge."

Washington (state), **USA.** *Washingtonian.* Historic nicknames and slang terms include *Washingtoniac* and *Evergreener.* *COMMON NICKNAME*: Evergreen State.

Washington, District of Columbia, USA. *Washingtonian.*

Washingtonian. Resident of the District of Columbia (not *Columbian*) or a resident of the state of Washington. The term is also used for a follower or admirer of George Washington.

Waterbury, Connecticut, USA. *Waterburian.*

Webfoot. Oregonian.

West Bank (Israel). *West Banker.*

West, USA. (Collective name for the eight mountain and five Pacific states, according to the terminology of the U.S. Census Bureau). *Westerner.*

West Australia (state), **Australia.** *West Australian* or the potentially derogatory *Sand-groper* (see entry for **Banana-Bender**).

Western Sahara (formerly Spanish Sahara). *Saharan;* also *Sahraoui.*

Western Samoa (Independent State of Western Samoa). *Western Samoan.*

West Germany. *West German.*

West Indies. *West Indian.*

West Sider. Resident of Manhattan's West Side; i.e., that area west of Central Park in New York City.

West Virginia (state), **USA.** *West Virginian.* Historic nicknames and slang terms include *Panhandler* and *Snake.*

COMMON NICKNAMES: Mountain State and The Panhandle State, after its particular configuration between the Ohio River and Pennsylvania.

Wichita, Kansas, USA. *Wichitan.*

Wichita Falls, Texas, USA. *Wichitan* shows up in print, but Texan C.F. Eckhardt points out that "folks from Wichita Falls are usually called 'folks from Wichita Falls' since Wichita Fallers sounds like they've had a mite too much and nobody likes Wichita Fallites or Wichita Fallians."

Winnipeg, Manitoba, Canada. *Winnipegger*, sometimes shortened to *Pegger*.

Winston-Salem, North Carolina, USA. *Twin Citian.*

Wisconsin (state), USA. *Wisconsinite*. Historic nicknames and slang terms include *Badger*.
COMMON NICKNAME: Badger State.

Wolverine. Nickname for person from Michigan, the Wolverine state. It is not as commonly used today as it was in earlier times. It was among the names defined in *Davy Crockett's Almanac of Wild Sports of the West, and Life in the Backwoods*, published in 1835, the year before he died. He wrote that the Wolverine was "the all-greediest, ugliest and sourest characters on all Uncle Sam's twenty-six farms, they are, in that nature, like their wolfish namesakes, always so eternal hungry that they bite at the air, and hang their underlips, and show the harrow teeth of their mouths, as if they'd jump right into you, and swaller you hull without salt. They are, in fact, half wolf, half man, and 'tother half saw mill."

Woolhat. Poor, rural person. The term took on a cast of bigotry when Herman Talmadge took over Georgia in the confused and disputed 1947 gubernatorial election with the support of his *woolhatters*. The press called it the "wool-hat revolt" after Talmadge started making the point that he could have 25,000 of his supporters on the State House lawn "any time I give the word." Talmadge fought for all-white primaries and supported the poll tax. Huey Long of Louisiana was described by *Life* magazine as an advocate of "wool-hat radicalism."

From the distinction made between the wealthy and aristocratic, who wore fur hats, and the commoner, who wore wool felt hats.

Worcester, Massachusetts, USA. *Worcesterite.*

Wyoming (state), **USA.** *Wyomingite.* Historic nicknames and slang terms include *Sagebrusher* and *Sheepherder.*
COMMON NICKNAME: The Equality State.

Y

Y, France. *Ypsilonien.* Y is one of the few towns in the world with a one-letter name. They also refer to themselves collectively as *Les Yaciens.*

Yahoo. An unmannered rustic from the race of degraded brutes in Swift's *Gulliver's Travels*. The term is derogatory but not always, because it is sometimes self-applied to people who feel left out. A 1932 letter to the editor of *Time* shows not only its use but also the derivative potential of the word: "Sirs: The 40-billion-dollar lesson which we hinterland Yahoos have learned since 1914 is to look twice at any international gold brick which Yazoos of New York and the Yapoos of Washington offer us."

Yank. *American.* This term tends to show up in Canadian and British newspapers.

Yankee. 1. Label used for residents of the New England states. 2. Label used for the residents of the Northern states at the time of the Civil War. In this context the term still has derogatory overtones when used in the South to describe the people of the North. 3. Label used outside the United States to describe Americans. Its applications range from the affectionate British use of the term *Yank* to the anti-imperialist slogan of the post-World War II era, Yankee Go Home.

The exact origin of this term defies detection. The file on *Yankee* in the Tamony Collection contains no less than eight etymologies. One of them, for instance, is that it came from the name *Jan Kaas*, which the British used to describe the Dutch freebooters in early New York. The Dutch in turn applied it to English traders in Connecticut and eventually *Jan Kaas* became Yankee.

Yanqui.*Yankee* in Spanish, which is pronounced as it is in English (yan-key). It is used in English to indicate a Latin American context; for instance, an article title in *The Economist* for December 5, 1987 reads, "Latin America's new democrats gang softly up on the Yanquis."

Yap (islands), **Micronesia.**   *Yapese.*

Yemen (The Yemen Arab Republic). *Yemeni.* This is also known as North Yemen. *Yemenite* is used occasionally. Charles Poe finds the term in use in Jean-Jacques Servan-Schreiber's *The World Challenge.*

Yemen (The People's Democratic Republic of Yemen).*Yemeni.* This nation is also known as South Yemen. *Yemenite* is also used on occasion.

Yoknapatawpha County, Mississippi, USA.   (The 2,400-square-mile county created by novelist William Faulkner and featured in his books.) *Yoknapatawphan.* The fictional county, populated by Compsons, McCaslins and Snopes, bears strong resemblance to Faulkner's lifelong home of Lafayette County, Mississippi.

Yonkers, New York, USA.   *Yonkersite.* In his 1936 *New Yorker* article on the subject, H. L. Mencken reported three factions had recently tussled over the preferred term. *Yonkersite* bested *Yonkers man* and the tonier Yonkersonian.

Yorkshire (county), **England, UK.**   *Yorkshireman/Yorkshire-woman.* The slang term is *Yorkie.* For a further explanation of *Yorkie* see the entry for **Lancaster.**

Youngstown, Ohio, USA. *Youngstowner.*

Ypsilonien. Resident of Y, France. They also refer to themselves as *Les Yaciens*.

Yucatan. Yucatec.

Yugoslavia (Socialist Federative Republic of Yugoslavia). *Yugoslav* or *Yugoslavian*. The CIA's *World Factbook* lists only *Yugoslav*, but many find it easier to say or write the alternative, as in "Bird Leads Celtics Past Yugoslavians" (sports page headline, *Washington Post*, October 22, 1988). See also *Jug* for a nickname that may be derogatory.

Yukon Territory, Canada. *Yukoner.*

Z

Zaïre (Republic of Zaïre). *Zaïrian*. This was formerly the Congo Republic (Kinshasa), before that the *Congo* and before that the Belgian Congo. *Zaïrois* is also used.

Zambia (Republic of Zambia, formerly Northern Rhodesia and from 1953 to 1963 part of the Federation of Rhodesia and Nyasaland; it became Zambia with independence in 1964). *Zambian*.

Zanzibar. *Zanzibari*. Now obsolete, as the nation ceased to exist in 1964 when it merged with Tanganyika to form Tanzania. In his fascinating article on how countries were named, Stephen Demorest pointed out, "The island of Zanzibar (once one of the world's most vile slave ports) got its name from the Arabic *zang* (black) plus *bar* (coast)."

Zimbabwe (Republic of Zimbabwe). *Zimbabwean*. This country was known as Southern Rhodesia and then Rhodesia during nine decades of rule by the white minority. In April 1979, the country became Zimbabwe Rhodesia after general elections. Later in the year, April 25, Rhodesia was dropped from the country's name. Zimbabwe (meaning "dwelling of the chief")

chief") was the name used for this area from the 15th to the 19th centuries. A nickname used for write Zimbabweans is *Rhodie*, which derives from Rhodesia.

Zonian. Resident of the Canal Zone in Panama, but almost always an American who resides there and works for the Panama Canal. *Zoniac* is a much less common alternative.

Zonie. Derogatory name for a resident of Arizona. Explained by Arizonan Michael A. Stackpole, "During August when it becomes unbearably hot here, many folks vacation in San Diego and there we are known as Zonies. This is not an affectionate term...."

Zürich, Switzerland. *Zürcher,* although *Webster's Ninth New Collegiate Dictionary says Züricher.*

Bibliography

A large part of the research for this book was done with the aid of hundreds of newspaper articles found in the Tamony Collection at the University of Missouri and various clipping morgues, including the old *Washington Star* files now at the Martin Luther King Library in Washington, D.C., and material on file at the National Geographic Library. Charles D. Poe of Houston provided several hundred citations from novels, newspapers and works of nonfiction.

In addition to the major unabridged and collegiate dictionaries, the books and articles that provided the most help in separating, as William Safire once put it, the *Whereveronians* from the *Whereverites*, *Whereverans* and the *Whereverers* are the following:

Adams, J. Donald. *The Magic and Mystery of Words*. New York: Holt, Rinehart and Winston, 1963.

Associated Press. *The Associated Press Stylebook and Libel Manual*. Edited by Christopher W. French, Eileen Alt Powell, and Howard Angione. Reading, Mass.: Addison-Wesley, 1980.

Bardsley, Charles Wareing. *English Surnames: Their Sources and Significance*. London: Chatto and Windus, 1906.

Beeching, Cyril Leslie. *A Dictionary of Eponyms*. London: Clive Bingley, 1983.

Berrey, Lester V., and Van Den Bark, Melvin. *The American Thesaurus of Slang*. New York: Thomas Y. Crowell, 1953.

Blumberg, Dorothy Rose. *Whose What?* New York: Holt, Rinehart and Winston, 1969.

Borgmann, Dmitri. "A Sociological Note." *Word Ways*, February 1986.

Bradley, Henry, and Bridges, Robert. *Briton, British and Britisher*. S.P.E. Tract Number XIV. London: Oxford University Press, 1923.

Brandreth, Gyles. *More Joy of Lex*. New York: Morrow, 1982.

——. *Pears Book of Words*. London: Pelham Books, 1979.

Brooke, Maxey. "Everybody Comes from Somewhere." *Word Ways*, August 1983.

Campbell, Hannah. *Why Did They Name It?* New York: Bell, 1964.

Central Intelligence Agency. *The World Factbook*. Washington, D.C.: General Printing Office, 1984, 1988.

Chapman, Robert W. *Adjectives from Proper Names*. S.P.E. Tract Number LII. London: Oxford University Press, 1939.

Ciardi, John. *Good Words to You*. New York: Harper and Row, 1987.

Collocott, T. C., and Thorne, J. O. *The Macmillan World Gazetteer and Geographical Dictionary*. New York: Macmillan, 1955.

Craig, Mary Stewart, "Do Mamaroneckers Like to Neck?" *Word Ways*, November 1987.

Davies, C. Stella, and Levitt, John. *What's in a Name?* London: Routledge & Kegan Paul, 1970.

Dawson, J. Frank. *Place Names in Colorado*. Denver: Golden Bell Press, 1954.

Demorest, Stephen. "A Lexicon of Countries." *Travel and Leisure*, September, 1981.

Dickson, Paul. *Names*. New York, Delacorte Press, 1986.

Dolan, J. R. *English Ancestral Names*. New York: Potter, 1972.

Eckler, A. Ross. *Word Recreations*. New York: Dover, 1979.

Eisiminger, Sterling. "A Glossary of Ethnic Slurs in American English." *Maledicta* 3 (1979), 153-174.

———. "A Continuation of a Glossary of Ethnic Slurs in American English." *Maledicta* 9 (1988), 51-61.

Espy, Willard R. *An Almanac of Words at Play*. New York: Clarkson Potter, 1975.

———. *Another Almanac of Words at Play*. New York: Clarkson Potter, 1980.

———. *Thou Improper, Thou Uncommon Noun*. New York: Clarkson Potter, 1978.

Flexner, Stuart Berg. *I Hear America Talking*. New York: Van Nostrand, 1976.

———. *Listening to America*. New York: Simon and Schuster, 1982.

Funk, Charles Earle. *Thereby Hangs a Tale*. New York: Harper and Bros., 1950.

Gannett, Henry. *The Origin of Certain Place Names in the United States*. Washington, D.C.: U.S. Geological Survey, 1905.

Gard, Robert E., and Sorden, L. G. *Romance of Wisconsin Place Names*. New York: October House, 1968.

Harder, Kelsie, B. *Illustrated Dictionary of Place Names*. New York: Van Nostrand, 1976.

Hook, J. N. *The Book of Names*. New York: Franklin Watts, 1983.

Jacobs, Noah Jonathan. *Naming Day in Eden*. New York: Macmillan, 1969.

Kane, Joseph Nathan. *The American Counties*. Metuchen, N.J.: Scarecrow Press, 1972.

Keaton, Anna Lucile. "Americanisms in Early American Newspapers." Dissertation, University of Chicago, 1933.

Lambert, Eloise, and Pei, Mario. *The Book of Place Names*. New York: Lothrup, Lee and Shepard, 1961.

———. *Our Names: Where They Came From and What They Mean*. New York: Lothrop, Lee and Shepard, 1961.

Laycock, Don. *"D'où Êtes-Vous?" Word Ways*, May 1986.

Lederer, Richard M., Jr. *The Place Names of Westchester County*. Harrison, N.Y.: Harbor Hill, 1978.

Loughhead, Flora Haines. *Dictionary of Given Names*. Glendale, Calif.: Arthur H. Clark, 1958.

McDavid, Raven, and McDavid, Virginia. "Cracker and Hoosier Names." September, 1973.

Manguel, Alberto, and Guadalupi, Gianni. *The Dictionary of Imaginary Places*. New York: Macmillan, 1980.

Marquis Bibliographical Library Society. *Liverpudlian*. Chicago, 1970.

Matthews, C. M. *English Surnames*. New York: Scribner's, 1966.

———. *Place Names of the English-Speaking World*. New York: Scribner's, 1972.

Mawson, C. O. Sylvester. *International Book of Names*. New York: Crowell, 1934.

Mencken, H. L. "The Advance of Municipal Onomastics." *The New Yorker*, February 8, 1936.

———. *The American Language*. New York: Knopf, 1919.

———. "Names for Americans." *American Speech*, December 1947.

———. *Supplement One to the American Language*. New York: Knopf, 1945.

Michaels, Leonard, and Ricks, Christopher. *The State of the Language*. Berkeley: University of California Press, 1980.

Mitchell, Edwin Valentine. *It's an Old New England Custom*. New York: Vanguard, 1946.

Moore, W. G. *A Dictionary of Geography*. New York: Praeger, 1969.

Morgan, Jane; O'Neill, Christopher; and Harre, Rom. *Nicknames*. London: Routledge and Kegan Paul, 1979.

Morris, William and Mary. *The Harper Dictionary of Contemporary Usage.* New York: Harper and Row, 1975.

National Geographic Society. *National Geographic Delimits Near, Middle and Far East.* News bulletin, April 27, 1952.

————. *Rules Look the Other Way When Names Are Coined.* News bulletin, May 19, 1948.

Newman, Edwin. *Strictly Speaking.* New York: Warner, 1975.

Noble, Vernon. *Nick Names.* London: Hamish Hamilton, 1976.

Noel, John V., Jr., and Beach, Edward L. *Naval Terms Dictionary.* Annapolis: Naval Institute Press, 1973.

Partridge, Eric. *Name into Word.* New York: Macmillan, 1950.

Payton, Geoffrey. *Payton's Proper Names.* London: Frederick Warne, 1969.

Pizer, Vernon. *Ink, Ark., and All That: How American Places Got Their Names.* New York: Putnam's, 1976.

Randolph, Vance, and Wilson, George P. *Down in the Holler: A Gallery of Ozark Folk Speech.* Norman, Okla.: University of Oklahoma Press, 1953.

Rayburn, Alan. "Of Hatters, Capers, Townies, and Trifluviens and other monikers people call themselves," *Canadian Geographic,* August-September, 1989.

Roback, Abraham. *A Dictionary of International Slurs.* Waukesha, Wis.: Maledicta Press, 1979.

Safire, William. *I Stand Corrected.* New York: Times Books, 1984.

————. "My Fellow Americans." *New York Times Magazine,* June 6, 1982.

————. *On Language.* New York: Times Books, 1980.

————. *Take My Word for It.* New York: Times Books, 1986.

Severn, Bill. *Place Words.* New York: Ives Washburn, 1969.

Shipley, Joseph T. *Playing with Words*. Englewood Cliffs, N.J.: Prentice-Hall, 1960.

Smith, Benjamin E. *The Century Cyclopedia of Names*. Four volumes. New York: Century, 1895.

Spaull, Herb. *New Place Names of the World*. London: Ward Lock, 1970.

Stacey, Michelle. "Names People Say," *The Chicago Reader*, October 21, 1983.

Stewart, George R., Jr. *American Given Names*. New York: Oxford University Press, 1979.

————. *Names on the Globe*. New York: Oxford University Press, 1975.

————. "Names for Citizens." *American Speech*, February, 1934.

————. *Names on the Land*. New York: Random House, 1945.

Tarpley, Fred. *Ethnic Names*. Commerce, Texas: Names Institute Press, 1978.

Tarpley, Fred, and Moseley, Ann. *Of Edsels and Marauders*. Commerce, Texas: Names Institute Press, 1971.

Treble, H. A., and Vallins, G. H. *An A.B.C. of English Usage*. Oxford: Oxford University Press, 1954.

Weekley, Ernest. *Jack and Jill: A Study of Our Christian Names*. Ann Arbor, Mich.: Gryphon Books, 1971.

————. *The Romance of Words*. London: John Murray, 1913.

Wells, Evelyn. *Treasury of Names*. New York: Duell, Sloan and Pearce, 1946.

Wells, Helen T.; Whiteley, Susan H.; and Karegeannes, Carrie E. *Origins of NASA Names*. Washington, D.C.: Government Printing Office, 1976.

Wolk, Allen. *Everyday Words from Names of People and Places*. New York: Elsevier/Nelson, 1980.

―――. *The Naming of America*. Nashville: Thomas, Nelson, 1977.

The "Word Wurcher" [Harry Partridge]. *"D'où Êtes-Vous Revisited" Word Ways*, August 1986.

Youmans, Charles L. *What's in a Name?* Lancaster, N.H.: Brisbee Press, 1955.

Naming Names— An Acknowledgment

A far-flung network of kindly, generous and knowledgeable people helped me with this book. I have taken the liberty of applying some appropriate demonyms in offering thanks and deep appreciation to:

Bavarian-Waukeshan Reinhold Aman
Canadian Jay Ames
Briton Roger B. Appleton
Kansas Citian Joe Arther
Londoner Russell Ash
Hoosier (and resident of Santa Claus) Joseph Badger
Philip W. Bateman
Larry W. Bryant
Virginian Monique M. Byer
Ottawan Phillip Chaplin
Missourian Gerald Cohen
Golden Stater David Conrad
Texan Ralph D. Copeland
Cantiburian David S. Cousins
Virginian Al deQuoy
Gordon B. Dean
Floridian S. Percey Dean
San Franciscan Charles F. Dery
John Duffie
Buckeye Russ Dunn, Sr.
Marylander Frederick C. Dyer
Texan C. F. Eckhardt
Missourian G. R. Edwards
Michael A. Emge

Willard Espy
Hoosier James E. Farmer
Washingtonian Michael Feinsilber
New Yorker Wayne H. Finke
Akronite C. H. Fleming
Barbara Rainbow Fletcher
Puebloid R. M. Gagliano
Walt Giachini
Washingtonian Tim Gibson
Thomas E. Gill
Washingtonian Joseph C. Goulden
Brooklynite Robert Greenman
Denverite Irving Hale
Gothamite Ralph E. Hamil
Kelsie Harder
N. Sally Hass
Bender John M. Hazlitt
Archie Edward Hinson
Littletonian Margaret Hoekstra
Columbian Lane E. Jennings
State of Mainer Warren R. Johnston
Venturian Leilani A. Kimmel-Dagostino
San Franciscan George Kirby
W. L. Klawe
Martin S. Kottmeyer
Washingtonian Bobby Kraft
Sarasotan Charles R. Lancaster
New Hampshirite Richard Lederer
Washingtonian Ray Leedy
New Yorker Ed Lucaire
Missourian Sue McCulkin
Siouxlander Michael McDonald
"Person from Sioux Falls" Bill McKean
Marylander Jack Mantel
St. Paulite John Vogt Masengarb
Oklahoman Susan Elizabeth Musick
Babylonian J. Baxter Newgate
John Ohlinger
Londoner Denys Parsons
M. K. Paskus

Milwaukeean Cate Pfeifer
Gothamite Louis Phillips
Shreveporter Robert Joseph Powers
Allan D. Pratt
Rainbow
Washingtonian Dan Rapoport
Nepeanite Alan Rayburn
Allen Walker Read
Englishman Ross Reader
Barbareno Ron Riopelle
Missourian Randy Roberts
Springfielder (Mo.) Charles R. Rosenbaum
Queenslander W.N. Scott
New Yorker David Shulman
Bostonian Bob Skole
Bob Snider
Phoenician Michael A. Stackpole
Washingtonian Linda Starke
Nutmegger Norman D. Stevens
Bethesdan J. O. Stevenson
Houstonian Rusti Stover
Kansas Citian Bill Tammeus
Nutmegger James Thorpe, III
Las Vegan Robert J. Throckmorton
OBtian Ellen Todd
Brooklynite Jonathan Tourtellot
Washingtonian Lillian Tudiver
St. Louisan Elaine Viets
Nick Webb
Minneapolitans Bob and Mary West
Northamptonian Emily Harrison Wier
Neal Wilgus
Virginian Ben Willis
Baltimorean Melvin H. Wunsch

Thanks once again. Also, should there be a future version of this book, the author is planning to keep an active file of demonyms and would like to hear from readers with comments as well as additions and corrections to the collection. He can be reached at Box 80, Garrett Park, Md. 20896-0080.